Ethics, Reason, & Excellence:
A Simple Formula for Leadership

Kevin Unruh

First published by Dog Ear Publishing
4011 Vincennes Rd
Indianapolis, IN 46268
www.dogearpublishing.net

ISBN: 978-1-45756-092-7

This book is printed on acid-free paper.

Printed in the United States of America

To my Dad

Contents

Introduction

In 2016, I was asked by executive management at the local office of the organization where I work to help develop a leadership program. It's a subject I have always been interested in and one that has always seemed intuitive to me. So, when I was asked if I could initiate the program and a presentation to kick it off, I, of course, said yes. And, after converting 20-plus years of mental notes to paper, I developed a half-day presentation which I gave to all the executives and supervisors in my office. This book represents a more comprehensive version of the original presentation.

After giving the presentation, which precipitated numerous follow-up conversations at the office, I became more aware – more focused, I should say – on just how much the topic of leadership arises in the course of an average day and how much of an impact leadership has on the everyday life of both employee and employer. Not too many things seemed more important than the topic of leadership, especially in the midst of work, so, after stewing on the idea for nine months or so and finally allowing a sense of compulsion to outstrip my feelings of reluctance in preparing to undertake a formal writing project, I decided that if I was going to put my preoccupations to rest, writing a book on leadership was my only real option. And, writing a book on leadership seemed to make more sense than not writing one, anyway – so here we are.

I have no desire, per se, to be considered an "author," nor do I have any designs on, nor even any hopes of making any money from this endeavor (although I do sincerely thank those of you who purchased this book). In fact, in publishing this myself, without any attempt to pitch it to a traditional publisher, I knew that I would probably lose money, in that I knew that recouping the publishing fees was unlikely – and I am fine with that. Recognition is not important to me. But, while my pursuit of notoriety may be rather relaxed, my ambitions of changing the culture in the ranks of leadership are not. There is power in words because there is power in thought, and all it takes sometimes for a concept or theory or formula to take root is for one person to say it and a few objective, well-meaning, thoughtful people to take notice – and to take action.

This book is but a humble attempt to plant a seed. And, as I write this, I find myself strangely confident that there are more than a few of you out there who will embrace the ideas set forth here and nurture this seed wherever you work, manage, and lead by applying the simple principles herein, with my primary objective being simply to help – to help employers and to help employees, by helping leaders.

And why not. We spend a third of our time at work (many of you even more than that), and the leadership, or lack thereof, where we work is an important factor in the degree of our happiness, and, sometimes, in whether we are happy at all. So, yes, I find a discussion of leadership especially worthy of my time. But I'm getting ahead of myself, I suppose. First, a little context.

As of this writing, I work at a large company with thousands of employees nationwide and about 600 employees at the local office where I am assigned. I have held numerous positions at this company over many years and in several different areas. I have been a supervisor, an advisor, a coordinator, a chairman, an educator, and a counselor, several of these at the same time.

Many reading an actual copy of my résumé would likely find enough justification for my writing on the subject of leadership. Others, of course, would not find credibility in anything less than a book written by the CEO of a *Fortune 500* company or by a leadership consultant that makes $2,000.00 per hour to come in and audit a corporation. I have decided, however, that the purists out there – those that are willing to accept wisdom at face value, regardless of the renown of the contributor – are those for whom I am writing. I freely admit that name recognition or a lofty title in industry might make my philosophies more marketable, but I do not think that such would make them any more logical, insightful, or sound. Take all the wonderful and wise quotations that have been collected over the last 300 years or so and remove from them the names of all the poets, presidents, and philosophers that spoke them and ask yourself if their words would be any less wise had they been spoken by people with no reputation at all. For those of you reading a book on leadership for all the right reasons, I am confident that any wisdom in this book, in and of itself, if delivered, will prove more valuable than any degree of prominence attached to the author.

One other thing. If there is truth in these pages, where I work and what I do aren't really relevant, so I've left out these details. I didn't want them to become even minor preoccupations to detract from the narrative. Further, my current employment serves as only a portion of the source of my observations and perceptions, and no part of it is a specific critique of my company or those with whom I work. I am fortunate to work at a good and meaningful place, and I am very happy in my position, having worked with many, many fine leaders and co-workers there, both past and present. Much of my analysis comes also from leaders I met in my fraternity and former jobs, and a great deal from conversations with family, friends, and associates about the topic of leadership, bosses, and general work life.

OK, back to the gist of things.

Good leadership has the ability to transform people's lives, organizations, companies, governments, societies – any place or entity where people are gathered in pursuit of a common goal. I believe wholeheartedly in the validity of the leadership formula I am presenting here, not because I think I am smart, but because I have seen irrefutable evidence that the formula works – anywhere, anytime, for anyone.

Though I address throughout this book leaders of "employees," I use this term in a generic sense only. This book is intended for anyone in any position of leadership, wherever there are people to be led. Whether you work at a large corporation, for a charity, are a coach, a teacher, a parent, the mayor, or just lead a group of individuals in your small town, I believe that the leadership principles discussed here aptly apply to all of you. I believe that the qualities and the principles of leadership are universal, and I believe by the end of this book, you will believe this to be true as well.

Leadership is simple. It truly is. It's not *easy*, mind you, but it is simple. My hope is that this book will convince you of this by providing you with a reliable and unifying formula that will ensure your success as a leader.

CHAPTER 1

The Right Thing

I was in a fraternity many years ago. I don't want to distract from the story by discussing too many details of this fraternity lest I get us all caught up in the inevitable biases of high-stakes, inter-fraternity politics (who is better than whom, and so forth). So, I hope it will suffice for me to say that it was a great fraternity, and literally, by all measures, the top one on campus.

Anyway, one Saturday afternoon at the fraternity, I was walking past the office of the newly elected house president when I popped my head in to say hello. He said hi, and, in a slightly apprehensive way, asked me if I had a minute to talk. I said of course and stepped in to talk to him about what appeared to be, based on the micro-contortions of his face, a relatively urgent concern.

With a humble but rather tense smile, he said, "I'm nervous."

"About what?" I asked, though I already knew, generally, that he was talking about being the new president.

"I'm not sure I know how to do this," he said.

"Sure you do," I told him.

"I do?" he asked. "Why are you so confident and I'm not?" he laughed uneasily.

"Because it's simple," I said.

"Well, that's a relief," he said. "So what do I do?"

I paused for just a second and said, "Do the right thing." [This was before the movie of the same name, by the way.]

He smiled again and laughed, even a little more confused than before. "That's it? That's all you've got? I thought you were supposed to be smart?" he pleaded, light-heartedly, but clearly hoping that the *real* wisdom I must surely have been keeping from him was about to jump out from behind this unhelpful charade.

"Well, think about it," I said. "What else is there?"

He continued smiling at me (he smiled a lot by nature), seemingly believing that I was still prolonging an already annoying joke. But, as he focused on the words and studied the seriousness in my face, he realized that he had heard the only answer he needed, no matter how unsophisticated it may have sounded.

"I'm not quite sure I know what you mean," he said.

"Yes, you do... In every decision you make as president, be ethical and logical and you will always do the right thing."

He paused for a second or two, then smiled at me with a sudden sense of illumination and said, "You're right."

"I didn't tell you anything you didn't already know," I said. "You just needed to hear there wasn't anything more to it." And that was the truth. He knew what to do and always did. He just needed the confidence that sometimes comes from a little outside reinforcement.

I was 20 years old, then, I think. I had thoughts and philosophies on the topic of leadership sometime before that, of course, but this was the first instance I can recall in which I declared my philosophies with any sense of structure.

After being asked to develop a presentation on the topic of leadership these many years later, I added the construct of *excellence* to the formula as a measure of thoroughness, dedication, and quality, which I am convinced is just as important as the other two pillars of my leadership philosophy.

Leadership is simple. It is. It's not necessarily easy, but it is simple.

So, if, as I assert, that leadership is simple, then why are there so many smart but poor leaders in the world? Well, you're in luck. That's the entire intent of this book: to explain what good leadership is by explaining how to do it right.

CHAPTER 2

Leadership Itself

If you ask ten people for a definition of leadership, you will most likely get a combination of many descriptions, all of which typically serve to define what a good *leader* is, which, of course, is relevant and important. However, for the time being, for purposes of this book, I would like to focus on a working definition of leadership itself, as opposed to a discussion of the traits that make up a good leader, the person. And while this may seem like unnecessary nuance, I think you will find this is an important distinction to consider, if only for the moment.

My definition of leadership is pretty straightforward: *Leadership is the responsibility of those "in charge" to lead their employees toward accomplishing a prescribed undertaking.* The concept is easy enough, but the *complexities* of leadership emerge when we begin to discuss the difficulties of leading a collection of diverse personalities toward that undertaking. And, therein, is the crux of it all, right? *People.*

People complicate everything. Many might argue that leadership in and of itself would be relatively easy if not for all the difficulties brought to bear on leaders by many, if not most, employees. My philosophy is that leadership is simple and is *sometimes* even easy, even in spite of people and all their many alleged complexities. Yes, *alleged,* for you see, I don't find people very complicated at all. But, I will get to that a bit later. For now, I want to focus on what leadership really is: the *responsibility* to lead.

If you are someone who has "signed up," as they say, to be a supervisor or manager of some sort, I believe you have a duty to also be a *leader*. If that isn't your arrangement with your employer and you were truly just hired to be an overseer, then so be it – no foul. But, my philosophy is that employees hired to supervise and manage are generally expected to lead as well. That's what this book is about – the *duty* of leadership, the duty to focus on your responsibility to lead so that there is a sublimation in the job description from supervisor to mentor, motivator, coach, role model, and, ultimately, to *leader*.

When I was young and riding in the car with my Dad, I would observe the way he drove and the things he said, as most kids do, I suppose, and I noticed what a calm, patient, and attentive driver he was. He was very vigilant and precise, but he was also smooth. He was focused but never in a rigid way and was not easily agitated. On the very rare occasion that he did become agitated with someone on the road that wasn't paying attention, he would say in a slightly elevated tone, "Drive the car, man." What he meant by this low-key admonition was that, instead of fiddling with something in the backseat or playing with the radio or looking out the window, the driver should've been doing his *main* job, which was to *drive the car*.

Most humans are selfish, self-absorbed. Most seem to think their *job* is to do whatever they are trying to do at the moment and to get wherever they are going and that driving the car is secondary. Going to the store, dropping off the kids, going to eat, to work, etc. is their primary focus, while listening to music, texting, talking on the phone, gawking at other drivers, and so on is secondary. The act of driving the car is often a distant third. My Dad's words were a reminder that a driver's main job, his *primary* responsibility is nothing less and nothing more than driving the car. While in the car, a driver should have no other preoccupations. As you have no doubt gathered, my perception of the responsibility of leadership is the very same.

If you agree to supervise and manage a group of people, your job is to lead these people in pursuit of the organization's mission. That is your job, your responsibility, and your duty – it is not to augment your résumé, get executive perks, or increase your 401(k) by way of an increase in title and salary resulting from a promotion. These things may all be legitimately obtained benefits, but they should not be the primary concerns of any bona fide leader, nor should they ever become preoccupations. Once you sign up to be in charge, your focus should be on that and nothing else. *Drive the car. Do your job.*

Another thing my Dad used to say whenever we were working on something together, such as playing sports, working with tools, or some other activity that required concentration in which he observed my skills not to be up to my potential was, "Think about what you're doing." He didn't say it in a scolding way. He said it in a literal way, meaning that I should very specifically and with deliberation think about what I was trying to accomplish. If I got frustrated while trying to throw an accurate curve ball, for instance, and it was clear I had lost my focus, he would ask me to stop and re-concentrate my efforts. "Take a second and think about what you're doing," he would say. Again, the message: *do your job.*

Both of these wisdoms of his, while they also clearly apply well to other circumstances, are especially well applied to the principles of leadership: being mindful of the responsibilities of the job and focusing on each aspect of doing it well.

Many managers I have observed over the years seem to believe themselves leaders because they have been placed in charge and/or because they have strong personalities. True leaders, however, are leaders because they focus their thoughts and actions on the act of leadership and on the essence of what it means to lead. True leaders weigh every decision they make against prescribed principles of leadership, instead of simply making decisions based on what feels right, what is convenient, what their personality impels them to decide, or worse, whatever serves their personal agenda. True leaders *do their job* and lead.

CHAPTER 3

Craftsmanship

L eadership, just like any other job, requires a few basics in order for the leader to be successful. I will discuss the traits of a good leader soon, but first I want to talk about the essentials, which are even more fundamental than the baseline personalities and behaviors that tend to constitute good leaders.

First and foremost, a leader must be dedicated to the *craft of leadership*. I cannot over-emphasize the importance of this particular philosophy. The entirety of this book depends on this premise: that commitment and dedication to the role of leader are paramount to leadership success.

We all know craftsmen that bring credit to their chosen field. Who among us hasn't bragged on a roofer, plumber, woodworker, landscaper, welder, painter, or some other highly skilled craftsman as "the best in town"? All of us expect people who practice a trade or a craft to be the best. And, if they're not, we don't hire their services, and we never recommend them to our friends. Yet, as far as I have observed over the years, the concept of "craftsmanship" in the realm of leadership isn't very common at all. In fact it's downright rare.

Men and women all over the country are put in charge and asked to lead, who, very often too late, are realized by the company and/or employees to be poor leaders, but who, for any number of greater or lesser reasons, are allowed to remain in their positions. Do we not all know of at least ten examples of this phenomenon over the course of our employment histories? So, why is it that we don't treat leadership as a craft in the same way we expect it in other professions? I believe the reasons are many, but for now – and I will get back to this analysis soon – the point is that we don't. And that's not good.

To be a leader, a true and excellent leader, a person must be as dedicated to his job as a boot maker or a glass blower, for example, is to his.

[Before I go any further, I want to take a moment to say that my use of "he" and "his" is intended as a gender-neutral convention and a simple courtesy to the reader. Yes, I could write "her," "his/her" and "s/he" when referring to managers and leaders, but the fact is, it is much easier to read a "he" than it is to read the other more cumbersome options, if one is willing to accept that the use of this pronoun is nothing more than exactly what I have stated it is. My use of "he" is not a social statement, and there is no agenda or implication in my use of "he" or "his." It is a pronoun without insinuation. I assure you I have known many good female leaders. I am simply avoiding clunkiness.] I continue…

Like the boot maker and the glass blower, a leader has dozens of different tasks he must perform daily in order to succeed in his craft. And, though the traditional craftsman works with a variety of materials and tools to perfect the object of his craft, a leader of men and women should be no less detailed and perfectionistic in attempting to guide his people to accomplish the mission of the day. Of course, I realize that the two jobs – craftsman and leader – are fundamentally different, but what I will not concede is that the two jobs are different philosophically. The same ideals, convictions, and attentions that make a premier boot maker also make an excellent leader. Until we start recruiting for and expecting from our leaders the same standards we expect from professional craftsmen, it is safe to say that the crop of good and effective leaders won't be any more bountiful than it is today.

But, sadly, at present, many of the so-called leaders filling the ranks of our companies are little more than supervisors or overseers, and some are barely more than babysitters. But, somehow we, as a society, have become content with this. Or, perhaps it is more accurate to say that we have simply become resigned to the fact that leaders are just hard to come by, that the pool of good contenders is just too shallow to produce meaningful numbers, and so we are forced to make do with what we have been given. How complacent; how defeatist; how tragic. My assertion, you have probably guessed, is that there must be a real change in our employment culture, a true *transformation*, in order for us to begin developing the leaders we need. This book is an attempt to start this revolution. Yes, I said *revolution*, and I'm not embarrassed that I did. I truly want to help make the world better for every employer and for every employee. Maybe this little book will light the fuse.

The average "leader" tends to get easily derailed from performing the functions of his job. Lack of preparation, lack of know-how, lack of focus, commitment, and dedication are all pitfalls of the average man or woman in charge. The boot maker and the glass blower cannot afford to be preoccupied with or impeded by such things, lest these things be allowed to corrupt the quality of their workmanship and, in time, doom their professional reputations. If leaders were treated as craftsmen, expected to behave as craftsmen, and if leaders comported themselves as if they were craftsmen, "leaders" would truly be leaders and the quotations marks could be removed.

Excellence is an art won by training and habituation. We do not act rightly because we have virtue or excellence, but we rather have those because we have acted rightly. We are what we repeatedly do. Excellence then, is not an act but a habit.

– Aristotle

A leader is someone charged with leading and guiding other people in order to accomplish a mission, and that, to many, sounds like a very difficult job. My ongoing assertion, however, is that it is not particularly difficult, if one is willing to take on the job with the same attitude as the person who chooses to make his craft his profession. If one has a sincere interest in the job, an aptitude (or a genuine willingness to learn), and the dedication to perfect the role as if it were a craft, the job is relatively easy to do well. *If.*

As I started to "hold forth" earlier, we spend a third of our lives sleeping, a third living life, and a third at work. How we feel about our bosses at work seeps into the other two portions of our lives, which makes a discussion of leadership about as relevant and urgent a topic as I can think of. As most all of us are either employer or employee, the condition of leadership at our place of work affects pretty much every-one, and that condition can be good, bad, or just so-so. Whatever the case, leadership is responsible for how we feel about life for no less than eight hours a day and often quite a bit more than that. That's a big deal. And because leadership is clearly one of the most significant social con-structs bearing on the human condition, I feel compelled to attempt to bring about a change in the way leadership is viewed – which I absolutely believe can be done, if you, the readers, will simply analyze this offering, and assuming agreement, do what you can to spread these philosophies, that is, discuss and model them, until there is a sea change (coming from the landlocked state of Oklahoma, I have absolutely no experience in maritime matters; however, I just couldn't bring myself to say "paradigm shift" instead) in what it means to be a "boss."

Some of you may ask, "Is this not a rather lofty goal?" Not to me it isn't. Any such goal justified and warranted by virtue of being commen-surate with the needs of the average employer and especially the average *employee* who depends on good leadership for sustaining his daily men-tal health and his financial well-being seems perfectly pragmatic. Ambi-tious? OK, but "lofty"? No, I don't believe so.

Indeed, the benefits of good leadership are many and weighty, so endeavoring to propose a purportedly culture-changing formula, while perhaps presumptuous, is, nonetheless, long past due. And with that, I present the most important part of the foundation: *commitment* to treating the role as a craft. Once an individual has the commitment and the dedication required to be a good leader, all that is left is the method, which can be synopsized in three words: *Ethics, Reason,* and *Excellence.* These, I am truly convinced, comprise everything that is needed for leadership to be effective, dependable, and honorable.

Influence, persuasion, negotiation, active listening, and other elements are all concepts that are commonly discussed in the context of leadership and are important to the general discussion. They are. But they are nothing more than words on a page, if one is not going to focus these principles as a dutiful leader on the good of the employee and the good of the organization. I'm sure any decent book on leadership will discuss these topics to a greater or lesser degree (in fact, even this one will), but without a dedicated effort to use these to facilitate both work-life improvements and production, they are of very little value – other than to sound as if you know what you are talking about.

I have read a few books on leadership over the last 20-plus years or so, and I skimmed a few more. No, that isn't very many for someone so interested in the topic. But, that's because most generally failed in my mind to truly answer the question and to answer it simply: "How does one do it right?" The ones I did read were well-written and well-received but none of them provided the unifying theory of leadership I was hoping had already been conceptualized. I am in no way suggesting that there aren't at least a few books out there that are truly fine contributions to the discussion of leadership. Hundreds, probably thousands, have been written and I am sure that many of them offer many good insights, instruction, and perspectives. I am saying only that I did not find what I was looking for in them. So, after being asked in 2016 to develop the leadership presentation I mentioned, I decided to write the book I never found, the one I wanted to read.

Inevitably, of course, there will be some of you reading this who can name a book or two that has some similarities to my philosophies and, if so, I am glad. I'm sure they are excellent and deserve reading. In developing my leadership presentation, however, I chose to base my assertions on my own philosophies and observations so that I would have the benefit of true conviction and enthusiasm as I spoke. My sincere and whole-hearted belief is that *Ethics, Reason,* and *Excellence* presents both a simple and unifying theory of leadership and, in its natural simplicity, also presents a set of ideas that are minimal in mechanics and process. Which is why this book is brief.

I did not set out to write a short book. It is brief because, as the title itself states, the formula for leadership is simple, and simple formulas should not require hundreds of pages to explain. Leonardo da Vinci said, "Simplicity is the ultimate sophistication," and I hope that philosophy is demonstrated here.

CHAPTER 4

The Formula

Many "leaders" I have interacted with or observed over the years failed before they even got out of the gate due to their lack of professional ethics. I'm not being moralistic here. I only mean that there are many ethics that apply to leadership – many of which are also common to everyday life – which leaders often fail to observe. *Ethics*, I believe, should be at the forefront of every decision that arises in a leadership environment in that they are at the heart of "doing the right thing."

Ethics are about principles, standards of behavior, taking the highroad and, with forethought, *doing* the right thing. And, true leadership is about making decisions based on these principles. Ethics, therefore, are not just ideas, things that we believe in, or things that we are; they are the ways and means by which we *choose* to act.

Putting one's ego before the mission, for instance, is a common example of less-than-ethical leadership. Putting one's personal interests ahead of the employees' is another common occurrence in leaders who lack a commitment to ethics. Failing to mentor, failing to motivate, failing to provide guidance, failing to care, failing to really lead employees in the right direction are all failures of ethics.

There is an almost endless number of circumstances in which ethics play a crucial role in the effective decision-making of leaders. As far as I can discern, ethics in decision-making are as important as the initial commitment that is required to be a good leader. I submit that at the core of every important leadership decision is an ethic to be considered, and often more than one.

Also at the heart of any important leadership consideration is *Reason*. Without ethics there can be no *good* decision, and without reason, there can be no *wise* decision. Reason is a standard of logic and common sense, examination, analysis, and ideally, wisdom, and it is a significant part of our everyday conversations in all walks of life. On a daily basis, somewhere in our social circles someone will eventually say, "that doesn't make sense," or "that doesn't sound logical to me." Logic is a fundamental part of human cognition. It's what makes science *science*, it adds ballast to human emotion, and it's the guiding force that makes things work out the way they should. Without reason, ethical decisions are merely good-hearted derailments.

Excellence in leadership is a commitment to greatness and superior service in this endeavor. It is a dedication to quality, efficiency, effectiveness, thoroughness, and to going "all in," to going above and beyond what is asked of you. It is the philosophy that good is not good enough and that only *great* will do.

The quality of a leader is reflected in the standards they set for themselves.

– Ray Kroc

Ethics, reason, and excellence are leadership pillars of principle and behavior that inspire those being led and encourage in them accountability by virtue of having a good example after which to model themselves. Leadership is little more than caring about what is right and causing others to care about the same things. In my mind, the simplest and best way to apply this philosophy and accomplish this objective is to devote yourself to these three domains, and the remainder of this book is a discussion of this formula as it is applied to the more common trouble spots of leadership.

CHAPTER 5

The Benefits

The benefits of good leadership are many. Good leadership brings morale, productiveness, and profit to the organization and consistency, happiness, and peace of mind to the organization's employees. Good leadership, I believe, is more important to morale and is a greater motivator of the common worker than almost any other aspect of an employee's work life. I don't have the numbers to prove it, but based on my own observations, I believe that high morale through good leadership is even more valued by employees than salary increases or workplace perks. Why? Because good leadership, more than any other factor I have observed, has the ability to cause people to enjoy coming to work, do a good job, remain loyal to the company, and to engage in productive behaviors while there. Money and perks typically give only short-term mood elevations. Sure, an unexpected raise in pay feels good at the beginning of the year, but the extra money rarely offsets the long-term effects of a bad environment. Real happiness at work, *sustained* happiness, comes from enjoying where you work and those with whom you do that work. Give an employee a good work environment and the average man and woman will be less likely to begrudge their pay, and a good leader, more often than not, is responsible for creating and maintaining that good environment.

The fundamental benefits of good leadership are hopefully obvious: it facilitates the accomplishment of the mission; it facilitates greater efficiency and greater production; it tends to engender people to the cause, whatever that might be; and, as noted, good leadership tends to make work life happier and better for all. Even if good leadership were responsible for happier employees and nothing more, this benefit alone would be enough to make a focus on leadership worth every effort. Happy employees, as we all know, tend to be good employees.

Good leadership can also be characterized as service-oriented. That doesn't mean servile or even deferential, for those who may be concerned by this word (service). It simply means that a leader is there to provide employees with what they need to forward the mission. Title is a license to *serve*, not a license to rule, and to this end, a leader should always be prepared and *available* to provide the following services to his employees:

- Coaching
- Teaching
- Mentoring
- Directing, guiding, illuminating
- Delegating, training
- Encouraging, impassioning
- Empowering, emboldening
- Supporting, championing, defending
- Providing for, facilitating

People may answer to a title, but they *follow* a leader. Employees may be forced to respect a title, but they will only truly follow a vision, a belief system, a set of principles, and a genuine person that embodies them. And, because there is no mission without employees, it is important to discuss what employees tend to respond to in a leader.

People follow men and women who are in charge because they –

- Trust them
- Feel a sense of loyalty to them

- Have respect for them
- Believe in their knowledge, expertise, and wisdom
- Like and admire them
- Feel compelled to emulate them

People *are* the company, people *are* the mission, so my leadership focus is squarely on the psychology of human nature. Which is also why I do not distinguish between the concept of management and the concept of leadership. I am aware of the distinctions made between the two in our business culture, and I accept that the distinctions often make a point (for example, "You manage things; you lead people." – Rear Admiral Grace Hopper). However, because people are at the center of every job there is (I hope no one is about to cite robots as an exception, as *people* still have to make them and fix them), even managing "things" is still about managing people, and I don't believe you can manage people without first leading them.

Another reason I don't care for the distinction between management and leadership is that some managers seem to want to choose which one they are best at naturally and resign themselves to being that one over the other one, instead of being both. There may be some nuance to the two concepts – I am willing to concede that – but as for a true dichotomy, I am not willing to go quite that far. Management without leadership is just supervision.

CHAPTER 6

The Anti-Formula

S ometimes, when examining what something *is*, it is important to also examine what it *is not*. For all good behaviors, there are bad behaviors; for any good formula, there is an *anti*-formula. And, as leadership formulas go, no matter which one you use, the anti-formula will always be any that substitutes the *Self*, a personal agenda, or anything that is antithetical to ethics, reason, or excellence. If these three components lead to good decisions, anything contrary to these will undoubtedly lead to poor ones. Try it. Look over the items below, all of which are in disagreement with the formula, and ask yourself how it could be possible to make a sound leadership decision by substituting any of these for ethics, reason, and excellence:

- Path of least resistance (personal convenience, avoidance of conflict)
- Self-preservation (insecurity, fear)
- Lack of understanding, common sense, expertise (laziness, incompetence)
- Vindictiveness, passive-aggressiveness, jealousy, competition
- Failure to ask for guidance (pride)
- Personal politics (self-centeredness, preoccupations)
- Apathy, lack of focus, lack of preparation (selfishness, laziness, lack of loyalty)
- Bending irresponsibly to outside forces (lack of courage)

- Failure to deliberate, rushing (lack of discipline)
- Over-reaction (fear, irrationality)
- Failure to delegate (micromanagement, fear)

Any of you who have ever had a boss have, undoubtedly, had most, if not all, of these *anti*-formula elements perpetrated against you and/or the company at one time or another. Hopefully, it is easy to see in this list that failures of leadership are failures of philosophy (ethics), analysis (reason), or follow-through (excellence).

Leadership is not only about doing the right thing, it is also very much about avoiding doing the wrong thing, and that takes commitment – commitment to self-awareness, commitment to detail, commitment to your people as individuals, and commitment to the craft. Leadership is not something you can wing. Leadership, *true* leadership, requires daily focus and contemplation. Your company and your employees deserve nothing less.

CHAPTER 7

Fear

There is no place for fear in leadership. *None.* Fear either biases perception, preventing one from assessing circumstances objectively, or disallows one from making the right decision in fear of the consequences. If one is going to be a true leader, one must have genuine convictions about the philosophies of leadership in order to benefit from the courage that naturally issues from such convictions. Real conviction affords ethical and logical adamancy, and there isn't a much more powerful position than knowing when you are right. But, the validity of this philosophy – "the courage of one's convictions" – is only as valid as the validity of the convictions themselves.

If we start with defensible leadership philosophies, test them over time, and continue to vet their validity and applicability, we can be confident that our decision-making matrix is sound. For me, confidence in leadership decisions comes from a fervent belief that the combination of ethics, reason, and excellence is the best formula for making these decisions. Fear simply cannot gain a foothold in the decision-making process when conscience, logic, and thoroughness are applied.

I should probably make a distinction, here, between fear and apprehension, doubt, and anxiety. When I make decisions based on these principles, I do not have fear or doubt that I am doing the right thing, in that my entire belief system is based on trying to do the right thing. However, I do sometimes have apprehension or anxiety with regard to how others might react to a particular decision. This apprehension is simply the cost of doing business, and I do not allow it to affect my decisions. It is normal to wonder if everything is going to turn out all right, of course, especially when others are involved. My point is that apprehensions about resulting reactions are just part of the game, whereas fear or doubt about making the decision itself should be a clear sign that either your "system" is unsound or your convictions are weak. Either way, something needs to be retooled.

Over the last many years, the very worst managers I have observed were the ones who were either mean-spirited or simply lacked courage. Even the ones that were not particularly skilled were still better than the ones that were unkind or insecure, or perhaps unkind and *prideful* is more accurate. I make this correction because managers that are insecure and *humble* tend to be receptive to criticism and, are, therefore, capable of self-improvement. But the combination of insecure *and* prideful is a bad one, for these two feed on themselves, making the combination more destructive than either of the two alone.

And the very *best* leaders I ever knew were fearless. In fact, as I pause to think on this statement, there was not a single boss I ever had that I would call excellent that wasn't confident, if not courageous. Confidence in one's self and one's abilities is imperative in a leader.

Fear and insecurity color every decision a manager possessing these makes. Everything such a manager does is made with an undertone, if not an unambiguous *overtone*, of self-doubt, anxiety, and dread. Fear is a powerful force, a very negative, debilitating, terrible force that permeates the daily life of anyone that is stricken with it.

I have known more than several managers who were insecure and fearful. They were not good managers, much less leaders. The decisions they made were based primarily on choices meant to avoid fear. They didn't choose something; they chose *against* something in order to escape feelings of distress. Instead of confronting the poor performance and conduct of a problem employee, for example, they simply avoided them or worked to transfer them to another area of the company. Instead of standing up for their employees, they conceded to upper management to avoid conflict. Instead of calling attention to a problem, they swept it under the rug for the next manager to deal with for fear of being punished for raising the issue. Fear and insecurity are cancerous. To everyone.

Employees, if you are fearful by nature, don't become a manager. You will not do well at it and you will be miserable. Employers, yes-men may appease you, but they can't and won't manage employees as well as those with the courage to stand on principle.

CHAPTER 8

Fear: Another Perspective

One of the very worst things a leader can do is to cause fear in his employees. Feeling fear is one of the most debilitating experiences humans must sometimes endure, and it is no less devastating and destructive in the workplace. Is there anything more agonizing than fearing one's supervisor, dreading going to work, or being worried about one's paycheck and the ability to care for one's family because the boss is an oppressor and a tyrant? I can't think of anything. Sure, leaders can get results from their employees through fear, but at what cost to the employee and to the company? And, what *greater* results could the same leader have achieved by using leadership principles instead?

Fear in the leadership ranks is even *more* destructive at the higher levels of management where it very naturally instills a toxic *cycle* of fear that affects employees at all levels. When the #1 boss is frightening, instilling fear consciously or otherwise, it makes the #2 boss afraid. When #2 is afraid, he will have a tendency to give instructions to managers below him based on his fear of #1. Bosses at level #3 will then make decisions and give instructions based on misguided advice they got from #2, who provided his guidance based not on ethics, logic, and excellence but on avoidance, the compulsion to please, fear of retaliation, etc. due to his fear of #1. Make no mistake, leaders: there is nothing worse than fear in the workplace. And just because your "numbers" look good doesn't mean you are a good leader or that your use of fear is effective.

Good people, good workers often do the right thing *in spite of* bad leaders. I have witnessed it many times. Fear does not inspire good work, nor does it motivate people, not in the long-term, anyway. In the long-term, all fear achieves, in any environment, is chronic dread and hopelessness, and I don't know anyone who would attempt to weave those into any credible theory of leadership.

I have discussed the topic of fear many times over the years with numerous managers seeking advice, and some, more naïvely than others (some not naïve at all), have stated that they were unaware that they were causing their employees to be afraid because, as they stated to me, that was never their intent. Whether there was a conscious intent or not, fear did pervade the leadership "style" of these managers, and it colored the majority of discussions these managers had with their employees. I know this because I also spoke to the employees who made this fact very clear to me.

Many times a leader didn't think he was "scary" because he didn't "yell," that he always tried "to be a nice person," that he tried to "give employees as much latitude as possible," and because he didn't "complain if people took long lunch breaks," for instance. In my discussion with these managers, I tried to help them realize that fear is not nearly as much about their intentions as it about the perceptions of the employees. If an employee is afraid, unless he or she is simply being irrational, the manager is usually to blame. My point to them was that fear is caused by many types of behaviors, some more subtle than others.

As a supervisor, as a *leader*, to avoid any misinterpretations, it is important to be aware of various behaviors that are common in managers and that cause anxiety or fear. For example, do you –

- Ask for counsel from an employee then argue with him?
- Begin shaking your head or interrupt before you have allowed the employee to finish speaking?
- Raise your voice?

- Scowl when an employee asks for time off even when they are entitled to it?
- Watch the clock, or ask others to watch it for you regarding employees?
- Tell employees asking for help to ask someone else?
- Feel threatened by new ideas, greater experience?
- Compete with subordinates?

And, even when these behaviors don't cause outright anxiety, dread, or fear, they do cause resentment, contempt, avoidance, distrust, and insecurity. These behaviors are very human, and sadly, very common. But, what is also human and common is for employees to learn from this behavior and to react timidly when in the presence of the offending manager or in the presence of *other* managers. People that get bitten by a dog in their youth will often come to fear dogs later in life. It's not very logical or objective, but it's not completely ridiculous either. Managers with these bad habits condition the same type of fear response in their employees, and although it is rarely intentional, the effects are just as damaging.

Leaders that are truly interested in receiving good counsel from their employees should take care not to make people tentative in expressing their opinions. I have witnessed many a meeting in which an employee with a good reputation, sound reasoning, and valuable insights has sat quietly for fear the boss might confront him harshly for having a dissenting opinion, or any opinion at all. Good leaders should not only want employees' opinions, they should expect them and ask for them routinely.

I have been just as guilty as others in believing sincerely that "people should know me well enough to know that I really do want to hear outside opinions..." But, what is unfair about this assumption is that while, perhaps, people *should* know that a particular manager may seem genuine in his willingness to listen, many employees may still be biased by past experiences in which former managers snapped at them, dismissed them, or otherwise made them to feel that expressing their opinions was not actually part of the program, as it were. Given the possibility of such bias, it is every leader's duty to make regular assurances regarding the welcomeness of others' perspectives. As a leader, you are, of course, not responsible for the first dog bite experienced by your employees, but you should feel responsible for ensuring that your employees never have to fear that they might get bitten again. This can only come about by creating a culture of safety and security in which the employees feels comfortable in providing counsel up the chain, freely and openly.

In this vein, ask yourself these questions. Do your employees feel safe in –

- Asking questions or seeking guidance from management?
- Recommending to management an opposing view for the good of the mission?
- Being frank and honest in their responses to management?
- Suggesting new ideas?

Now, please ask yourself whether you merely tolerate these or actively encourage them.

The best leaders debate with ideas and not with their egos or personal agendas. "Leaders" who debate to win are really just arguing, and arguments are almost always won by the man or woman with the highest rank. This is not leadership. True leaders debate to understand. They debate to listen, to learn, and to increase their base of knowledge pursuant to making a better decision. A discussion, even a debate with an employee, should never turn ugly. I have debated with many a supervisor in my time, many of whom were secure enough in themselves to debate without feeling that their title was being challenged. Those leaders were the ones I always felt comfortable bringing ideas to. Those leaders are the ones that benefitted from their employees' knowledge and insights because they were open-minded and humble enough to listen without annoyance or anger. Though I didn't win every debate, obviously, I always came back to discuss things because I felt welcomed and respected. I am very grateful to these managers because they were kind, they served as role models to me personally, and they honored the company by listening to other opinions instead of relying solely on their own.

I have also had a few bosses that considered almost all debate an act of confrontation and defiance. Those managers scared me. They scared me because I knew that it was not necessarily safe to have and express my opinions honestly. These managers made me gun-shy, afraid of causing them to become angry at the mere suggestion of a differing opinion. I dreaded meetings with these managers because I was never sure which of my opinions or suggestions might upset them. Consequently, I tended to avoid frank discussions with them, which is something a leader should never cause in an employee.

We all know lots of people that dread going to work. There are many reasons for dreading going to work, of course, but one common reason is feeling intimidated, anxious, or even fearful of interactions with one's boss. A good work environment, on the other hand, one that feels safe, is one that fosters a sense of hope and comfort, and any leader that can bring about such an environment is one that employees will trust, admire, be grateful for, feel camaraderie with, will support and serve, and be loyal to.

As a leader, these attributes – confidence, perseverance, work ethic,
and good sense – are all things I look for in people. I also try to lead by
example and create an environment where good questions
and good ideas can come from anyone.

– Heather Bresch

CHAPTER 9

Courage

Of all ethics, I easily put courage at the front, for it is courage that allows us to apply standards of integrity, and it is our integrity that justifies our courage. Before you can have courage, you must know who you are, what you stand for, and what you truly believe in – those things are your ethics. Once you have your ethics in order, making decisions as a leader, or just in life in general, isn't all that difficult. But, when *living* your ethics becomes challenging, only courage will make it easier. And you can only get real courage when you know you are right.

Have you ever seen how adamant someone is who has just been wronged? Have you ever tried to argue with someone who everyone knows is right? When people are in the right, they have unflappable courage. They do not concede, compromise, or wither. It is easy to be courageous when you are right. So, being right, that is, being blameless, honorable, on logical footing, and so forth, should always be the goal.

Do you know who you are? Do you truly believe in what you say you believe in? Is what you claim to stand for something you are willing to actively defend, willing to champion, or is it just a credo you claim belief in when appearances matter? I'm not being argumentative or mocking. I am sincerely asking you if you have taken inventory of your belief system and if you truly know what you believe in. If you haven't, it's time. You cannot be a leader without this foundation:

- Decide what you believe in on a given topic and do everything possible to make sure you're right
- Once you decide *where* you stand, *take* a stand – don't compromise and keep persuading those you are trying to lead (until, of course, such time as better logic, a better way, or better, clearer ethics present themselves)
- Take note of your success in *not* compromising (courage grows from success in your choices)
- Take time to map out the rest of your beliefs *before* you find yourself in need
- Make courage a habit and not just something you call up when things are dire

Courage is the most important of all the virtues, because without courage you can't practice any other virtue consistently. You can practice any virtue erratically, but nothing consistently without courage.

– Maya Angelou

It is my perception and belief that people are "born" with varying degrees of a given personality trait. I suspect many of you believe the same thing. We have all observed in very young children that some are more outgoing than others, some more humorous, some more courageous. It is unlikely that these characteristics were *learned* at the age of four, let's say, so it seems probable that these traits were assigned, as it were, by genetics. And while a person may be imbued with a strong measure of a particular personality trait at birth, making the development of that trait over time easier than it would be for someone with less of a predisposition, I would argue that these same traits can be *strengthened* with focus and effort, regardless of how much of that trait may have been bestowed on them at birth.

Many people lament that they are too shy to be good public speakers; others say they aren't very good in group settings because they lack social skills; some claim they aren't good leaders because they lack confidence. Of all these people, I would ask the same question: "What have you done to try to conquer your perceived inadequacies?" "What have you done to fix your shyness?" "What efforts have you made to improve your ability to interact with people?" "Have you attempted any exercises that might serve to increase your level of confidence as a potential leader?"

As has been discussed, it is undoubtedly true that some people are born to lead, but it is also true that those not given the gift of natural leadership can learn the necessary skills to become a leader, if they are willing to make a concerted effort to do so. All it takes is courage, focus, and determination.

Many of you reading this may be thinking that the courage part is the hardest part of the prescription. I agree. It is. If you were not given a large measure of courage early in life, then generating it later in life probably sounds rather difficult. But you're in luck. If you are the type of person that cares enough to read a book on leadership, it is likely that you have the character to improve your quotient of courage, which, I am convinced, is not nearly as difficult as you may think.

Courage and confidence are not the same thing, obviously, but there is a component of courage that includes confidence. And like courage, some confidence comes from predispositional gifts. Confidence also comes, though, from the assuredness we get from our own self-observations, from witnessing and analyzing our own successes.

In the realm of sports, for example, it is easy to gain confidence in your skills, if it is clear that your skills are as good as or better than the people you are playing against. Similarly, in the philosophical realm – whether we are discussing the philosophy of raising children, education, counseling, politics, or any other discipline – measuring success is arguably less clear and definitive. Still, the proof is in the pudding.

Confidence in your particular philosophy increases with proof that the precepts of your philosophy bring about greater understanding and success – the greater the success, the greater confidence you may have in your belief system. Confidence in leadership is exactly the same. If your belief system works, if it is clear to you and to others that it leads to success, the more confidence you can justifiably have in your system. More confidence, more courage.

Failures in leadership, as mentioned earlier, are very often due to a poor philosophy, a poor system of leadership (or the complete lack thereof), or due to a failure to faithfully adhere to a *good* philosophy of leadership. Failures of the first sort are failures of intellect or effort; failures of the second sort (failing to be true) are failures of integrity and ethics, which are ultimately failures of courage. Without courage, there can be no leadership. It is fundamental and crucial to any leadership philosophy. Courage provides the foundation for the formula and gives strength to the pillars that support it. Those that endeavor to follow the principles of ethics, reason, and excellence – whether they use these terms or not – will succeed as leaders. Those that falter as leaders will undoubtedly fail under the collapse of one of these three pillars. If there are exceptions to leadership failures outside these three, I have not observed them.

It is pretty easy to write forcefully about courage. Most everyone I can think of would agree that it is a good thing in almost all situations, so it isn't terribly difficult for me to champion the cause of courage, especially in the domain of leadership. That said, I am very aware that writing about it and extolling its inherent virtue is much easier than actually putting it into practice, which leads me to an important aspect of courage we need to talk about: *sacrifice*. Courage often requires it, especially in a leadership environment in which one is not at the top of the hierarchy.

When you are the "head man in charge," in a business setting, for example, having courage isn't particularly difficult. In fact, when you're the #1, courage is many times not even very relevant because you have the final decision on most things such that courage is not a great need (who needs courage, when you only have to convince yourself?). This section, however, is for those of you that are managers of employees but who also answer to a manager higher up than yourselves.

Making a decision that your boss won't or doesn't agree with, depending on his or her character, is a circumstance fraught with worry and potential trouble. Once you become aware that your decision is going to be questioned, you have only two choices, really: you can concede and reverse course, or you can try to win him over.

No one likes to debate with a boss, much less argue with one. It is often unpleasant, nerve-racking, and forbidding, if not forbidden. That's just the way of the world. People like to be right – it's human nature. Most people especially dislike realizing someone else's idea is better than theirs. Having a superior title, as we have all observed with frustration and disappointment, seems to make the level of this type of irritation even more bothersome for the superior title holder. It may not be fair, rational, or mature, but it's a reality we must contend with and endeavor to negotiate to the advantage of the mission, if we are to deserve being called a "leader." If ethics, reason, and excellence have invested you with the vision of the "right" decision, it is your duty to sell that vision up the chain. That's leadership. The concept of *sacrifice* comes into play when opposition from above looks to get in the way.

Disagreeing with the boss sometimes has consequences. It will more likely than not be uncomfortable and awkward. Unless the boss is unusually gentle, humble, and secure, there may be anger, elevated voices, maybe some bullying, maybe even some yelling, but the odds are that it isn't likely to be pleasant. If you are going to be a leader, I mean a real-deal, dedicated-to-the-craft, duty-bound, high-road, all-in type of leader, bearing up to this opposition and angst requires more than confidence, toughness, or tenacity. It requires sacrifice. And sacrifice is often painful.

When you disagree with a superior, you may risk damage to the relationship, you may risk loss of *political capital*, as goes the phrase, and you may risk losing trust, goodwill, and general supportiveness. Depending on the superior, you may even risk a demotion or losing your job altogether. To this last apprehension, I must interject here abruptly. If you fear getting fired for disagreeing with the boss in a professional manner, it is long past time to move on. It is not possible to be a true leader at a place where being honest and forthright is cause for termination. So, with all this at risk, it is clear that the sacrifice a leader sometimes has to make is the sacrifice of *Self*. Which is why the otherwise "good boss," the every day, "decent guy" supervisor tends to fail his people when the chips are down: because he is unwilling to stand his ground and sacrifice himself for the good of the order – not sacrifice his employment, you understand, but his *Self*.

The *Self* I'm talking about is composed of the things that make up the self-aware, self-conscious man or woman: primarily ego and emotion. And what is the cost of this sacrifice? Predominantly the pain and burden of fear, which is arguably the most upsetting and disruptive emotion on the spectrum.

When experiencing fear, the average person moves away from the source of that fear, whatever it might be – human nature, common sense, basic insecurities, or the instinct for self-preservation. The average person who sees that his boss is about to get upset due to a disagreement in philosophy, action, or otherwise, tends to defer, concede, or reverse direction. We humans just don't react well to fear. Our instinct for self-preservation is very strong, and it is very often stronger than our courage and our often tenuous sense of self-sacrifice.

The role of a soldier and the role of a parent both require sacrifice and responsibility. This is known "going in," as they say. So, it is rather difficult to sympathize with a soldier, for example, who might bemoan the level of his pay in proportion to the risk that he might get wounded or killed. Part of what it is to be a soldier, obviously, is putting himself in harm's way for the sake of the country he serves. It is expected that he will do this willingly and without complaint when the time comes because he chose the job – and that *is* the job. He knew that when he signed up. Parents are beholden in the same way. One isn't particularly justified in complaining about how much it costs, how emotionally draining it is, or how thankless it can be to raise a child because *that's the job*. That's what parents sign up for. And if you don't want the responsibility, if you don't think the job fits the pay or the risk or the frustration, then the obvious response is "Then don't take the job."

I view the responsibility of leadership in the same way. Leaders don't get a pass when the going gets tough. They don't get to pick and choose when they feel committed to standing by their duty. Ethics, reason, and excellence are responsibilities that go with the territory. If you are asked to lead and you take the job, it is your obligation to stand firm. Soldiers get shot at, but they stick to their guns. Parents sometimes get disrespected, but they continue to nurture and mentor. Giving up is not an option in either role. Bullets and dealing with childish behavior are part of the job description. So sometimes is disagreeing with your boss, if you are going to be a true leader. It's a sacrifice of *Self* you must be willing to make. That's the job, and you signed up for it.

A leader is one who, out of madness or goodness, volunteers to take upon himself the woe of the people. There are few men so foolish, hence the erratic quality of leadership in the world.

– John Updike

Which brings me to my final point in this chapter: Try never to go to work in the role of a manager for someone you know in advance does not share or agree with your philosophy of leadership. If you do this, any sacrifices of *Self* that you may choose to make will more likely than not, sooner or later, lead to your demise.

If your boss is self-centered and you are ethics-centered, how can you possibly succeed? There are only two answers to this. The first answer is that you can't. The boss will not understand you, will probably dislike you, and will contradict, if not controvert, your efforts to lead. The second answer is that you actually *can* succeed, but only if you persuade him that your leadership philosophies, while they might not be similar to his own, are working and are working for the good of the company. If the boss is half-wise, he will leave you alone. But, frankly, it is not very likely. So, when choosing a job and a position, make your belief system known and find out if your boss shares the same beliefs. If he doesn't, you are probably in for a very rocky road.

It turns out that this is the longest chapter in the book. I didn't plan it that way, but there is a reason that's the way it worked out. Where leadership is concerned, courage is the greatest ethic there is. Without it, there is no leadership.

CHAPTER 10

Rightness

S o, how do you know if you are doing it right or not? That's a tough one. I admit it. Obviously, people in positions of leadership have their decisions second-guessed on a regular basis. I have seen this a thousand times, and I have engaged in the practice myself. Everyone has an opinion; therefore, it is difficult to say unequivocally that one's decisions are the right decisions. Or is it? As I see it, it is *very* possible to make the right decision, no matter how many alternate interpretations there may be.

As I make decisions from a leadership perspective, I ask myself these things in an effort to adhere to my leadership principles, in concert with the formula of ethics, reason, and excellence:

- Is it just, fair, and honest?
- Is it objective?
- Is it prudent?
- Is it likely to be effective?
- Is it responsible and conscientious?
- Is it smart, wise?
- Does it weigh all the facts?
- Does it weigh all reasonable opinions?
- Does it serve the employee and the company?
- Is every aspect of this decision based on good intentions?

- Have I excluded from the decision-making process all personal agendas, motives, and biases?
- Is it likely to bring about the very best result, yield the highest performance, produce the most excellent product?

If all these things can be answered positively, then the decision will be *right* far more often than not.

But what if later it is learned that the decision was actually a poor one, not that it was not righteous, but that it was flawed in some way due to a lack of information, for instance? In that case, a good leader should do a few things: make note of any faulty logic that may have led to the decision; make note of the source of *new* facts that were not incorporated or available originally; and, most importantly, make immediate corrections. The formula I have offered up doesn't guarantee a perfect outcome every time, but it does guarantee a virtuous one. So, even when a good leader makes a decision that turns out *not* to be so good, the leader can still make things right by having the courage and humility to make adjustments and corrections. Even good leaders make mistakes, but when they do, they fix them quickly, without pausing to allow their egos to try to convince them they really didn't slip up. Making mistakes is part of the job. It is an absolute inevitability. But mistakes are never permanent, if a leader is always willing to put mission before ego. Sometimes it just takes two or three decisions, with a modification here and there, to end up in the right place.

CHAPTER 11

Have you ever?

I have known many managers over the years that claimed to believe in holding poor performing, "bad" employees accountable only to see them give those bad employees good performance reviews or even recommend them for promotion later. I have known these supervisors to elevate performance reviews to avoid confrontations, to avoid the work of correction and rehabilitation, to avoid criticism, to avoid legal challenges, or the irrational fear of career derailment, all while knowing that what they were doing was unethical, dishonest, and irresponsible.

As a leader, you are charged with the responsibility of running your department, all aspects of it, for the good of the organization and the good of the employees you lead. That is a lot of responsibility that many managers don't take very seriously for a variety of reasons. It is easy to lead good employees but rather difficult to lead bad ones. Nonetheless, as the person in charge, you are not allowed to cherry pick your duties, although a good many managers I have observed over the years do just that, choosing to do the easy stuff and avoiding the difficult. But, true leadership is about consistency, thoroughness, focus, dedication, and duty. Leadership, just like soldiering and parenting, has benefits, but it comes with a lot of detriments as well. Committing yourself to treating each duty with equal dedication and responsibility is the difference between a half-hearted supervisor and true leader. To illustrate this dedication, or lack thereof, it might be helpful to run down a few examples by asking yourself these questions:

Have you ever –

- Chosen to pass off a bad employee to someone else rather than making an effort to correct his behavior, or, if not feasible, to fire him?
- Chosen not to address bad conduct in an employee, hoping that he would quit or retire instead?
- Simply ignored employee problems because you were either intimidated by the problem, too stressed or tired to deal with it, didn't feel you were being paid enough to have to cope with it, or just put it off, hoping it would eventually just fade away?
- Failed to broach an important but delicate topic with a superior for fear of causing yourself problems?
- Agreed with a superior even when you knew he was wrong?
- Taken the easy way out by asking employees to tolerate negative conditions instead of working to correct the problem?
- Punished an employee because of your own failure to train/lead?

If you have, you were shirking your duties.

True leaders consider the responsibility of leadership to entail much more than just *leading* the pack. True leaders are shepherds, protectors, defenders, referees, mediators, coaches, torch bearers, role models, emissaries, supporters, teachers, mentors, trainers, comforters, and correctors. True leaders do it all. And that's why people follow them.

CHAPTER 12

Micromanagement

E mployees hate being micromanaged. I'm an employee and I don't like it when it happens to me either.

Typically, the act of micromanagement arises from just a few sources of uneasiness. It stems either from a need for excessive control and/or the lack of trust in one's employees work product or from the belief that your standards are higher than that of your employees. We all know what micromanagement looks and feels like, so I won't spend time on the obvious. It is frustrating, annoying, and maddening. However, there are times, in my opinion, when it is justified. This chapter is about those times, but it is also about when to turn it off.

If you already acknowledge that you are a "control freak" or that you have significant trust issues, it is time for you to go talk to someone that can help you attenuate those feelings and resulting behaviors. Good leaders do not micromanage. But, if you are *compelled* to micromanage because your standards truly are higher than your employees' or because you have a significant number of less-than-competent employees, which you must necessarily supervise with hyper-vigilance, then your circumstances qualify for a *temporary* period of micromanagement.

If your employees do not embrace your standards (*reasonable* standards), which causes you to have to follow behind them and make corrections to their work, I must tell you that this is a failure of leadership. Part of being a leader is causing employees to adopt your standards and beliefs. If they do not believe in what you believe in, if they do not perform at the same levels at which you perform, they are not really following you. Your job, your duty as a leader, is to do whatever is needed to trigger the adoption by your employees of your work ethic and values. Until you can accomplish this, you will always feel the need to micromanage.

Now, some of you might suggest in leadership that sometimes, given the difficulties of dealing with various employees, micromanagement is just part of the job, that it's just part of what they are paying you for. What I would argue, however, is that while you may be *willing* to micromanage, and while your extra efforts in doing so may seem generous, even magnanimous, they are mostly misguided. Long-term micromanagement is never healthy. Micromanagement takes time and effort that good leaders should not have to expend for protracted periods of time.

The second condition, when it is temporarily acceptable to engage in micromanagement, is when the employees working for you are so ill-equipped or unyielding that they cannot or will not meet reasonable standards of performance. In this case, as someone in a position of responsibility, it is arguably your duty to micromanage these employees – but only until they can be replaced or rehabilitated. Again, micromanagement should never be long-term. If as a leader you are unable to engender your principles in those you lead, or if you have employees that are unwilling or unable to meet your standards, then it is your responsibility to see that they are replaced with employees that are both. Micromanagement may feel like the right thing to do at the time, and sometimes it is, but a good leader will always be looking to put an end to it as soon as it is feasible.

There is a third condition in which micromanagement often occurs that is important to note. Managers that are not very comfortable at delegating (I have often been one of these) sometimes micromanage the employees to whom they have just turned over the reins on a particular project. The best way to address this tendency is to follow one simple rule for delegation: delegate to employees that are able to do the work. If they are not able to do the work, train them until they are, then delegate.

Delegating work to unready employees is poor management and will cost you twice the time and effort that it would've taken to do it yourself. One of the responsibilities of a leader is to train future leaders and delegating responsibilities to other employees is good for you, good for them, and good for the company – if they are ready. It is your job to get them ready. Once they are ready, delegate and walk away. The cardinal sin of delegating is following up behind with micromanagement. Doing so is annoying, at the minimum, and demoralizing, at the maximum. If you trust the employee, let him or her work. If you don't, then your training of that employee is not yet complete.

CHAPTER 13

Anger and Confrontation

A word about anger.

Yes, it is okay for leaders to get mad. No one expects you to be a robot. Besides, *righteous* indignation is a powerful force. On the other hand, temperance is also a powerful force – perhaps more powerful. Righteous indignation may manifest itself in anger, but as we know, anger often causes fear and aversion.

Humans are emotional. When we care about things and those things go wrong, we often get upset, frustrated, and angry. That's normal – happens to the best of us. But the important thing about getting angry, as a leader, is not whether you become angry or even about how often. It is about how you choose to express it.

I always thought it was odd when someone who was clearly angry denied being so when asked if they were angry. I know there are several reasons why people do this. I'm just saying I think it is rather phony. Why not just admit what is already known?

In interacting with employees during times when I have been angry, one technique I have used is stating openly that I am angry. Doing this serves two purposes: it adds transparency to the conversation, a sense of honesty, and it somehow mitigates the negative impact of the anger by

adding a measure of control to it by virtue of its being expressly acknowl-
edged. *Saying* you are angry is somewhat less intimidating to people than
simply *being* angry, and any attempt to diminish feelings of intimidation
is always worthwhile. It's okay to get angry sometimes. Just don't be
afraid of saying so out loud.

Many managers – I suspect most – allow negative feelings they may
have towards an employee to fester long before they decide to say anything about it. And, usually, by the time they do say something, they
have typically ramped up their resentment to a degree much higher than
it would have been had they addressed the issue as soon as it appeared.
Brooding, seething, and dwelling on a personal matter will affect every
interaction you have with that employee until the matter is resolved. If
you are upset with an employee who came in to work inexcusably late,
sent an unprofessional e-mail, or caused trouble with another employee,
for example, the wise thing to do, as we all know, is to address the matter right away. If you don't, it is only natural for your future dealings with
that employee to be tainted by your frustration with that person. This
habit in our work culture of putting off confrontation may be so com-
monplace as to seem inconsequential, but it isn't. If a manager spends
eight hours a day with that employee and does not attempt to resolve the
issue and his feelings about things, the employee will consciously or subconsciously tally each strained interaction with that manager, creating a
negative memory and a destructive emotional record for each contact he
has had with the manager, and the fact that the employee might be "in
the wrong" is not very relevant to this point. Whether the employee is the
cause of the manager's anger or not, it is incumbent on the manager, *as
a leader*, to arrest the momentum of that anger by addressing the problem with the employee before too much ill will has had the chance to
build up and impede the flow of good, honest, courteous communication.

I think of this relationship as a pipeline that is the responsibility of
the leader to maintain, to keep free of sediment and debris that collects
in the line between the manager and the employee when too many

instances of conflict have been left unaddressed. Confrontation of unprofessional or irresponsible conduct in an employee is unpleasant for most managers. But, a good leader stands watch over the channel and keeps it flowing freely, confronting any interpersonal flotsam and jetsam as it occurs, removing it immediately, rather than waiting until it is completely clogged before mounting a clean-up effort.

I've only met a few people over the years that seemed to take pleasure in confrontation (but then, they had issues…). Everyone else seems to hate it. No *normal* person enjoys feeling angry, frustrated, ramped-up, or resentful. But, confrontation does not have to be so ugly. I'm not claiming that confronting and correcting an employee will ever be pleasant, but it needn't be so dreadful that it causes us to put it off for days, weeks, or even months, and make our head, neck, back, stomach, and face hurt. So, my guidance on confrontation has been the same for many years: *Do not delay*. The longer you wait, the angrier you will get. The angrier you get, the less articulate and focused and professional you will appear and be.

People tend to fall into three categories when it comes to this type of procrastination. The majority of people, it seems, put off dealing with personnel issues for the same reason they put off washing the dishes, mowing the lawn, or painting the house: they just don't want to do it because it's unpleasant. The second group is composed of those who are "not very good at it," believe "it won't do any good," believe if they wait long enough "it will go away," or claim that it "really isn't my style." The rest of the people put off confrontation until their anger reaches an amplitude that *impels* them to confront the situation. By this point, their frustration has all but boiled over and they feel they no longer have a choice in the matter, feeling as if they are physically driven to confrontation by the crescendo of their emotion. I know a lot of people like this. And though I do not believe that most of these people *deliberately* wait until their anger is so elevated they feel compelled to act, I do believe (because numerous people have admitted this to me) that they dread confrontation so much that their subconscious coerces them to wait until their anger potentiates their motivation enough that a conscious decision to confront the employee is no longer necessary and they simply react. And, although the mind-body reaction may reduce the *initial* anxiety one gets from anticipating the confrontation and deliberating it, I'm sure I don't need to point out that what comes of this reaction and the corresponding delivery is usually far less cogent in the manager's speech and far less well received by the employee than it would have been had the confrontation transpired in the early stages of consideration. Anger is human. It's normal. And there are times when anger is perfectly acceptable in the workplace. But, instances in which confrontation is needed are not the best circumstances under which anger should be nurtured. Anger is often expeditious in that it can get the job done quickly ("Go out to the warehouse and fix your screw up right now!"), but composure is almost always more productive. Is it more important to you to be *fast* or effective, *right* or effective, *in control* or effective? Do your best to put principles over emotion.

Anger in its place and time may assume a kind of grace. It must have some reason in it and not last beyond a minute.

– Charles Lamb

Another technique I have found to be effective is using expressions of disappointment instead of expressions of anger. In a way, expressing disappointment is a sublimated form of anger. Anger is the outward expression, but the internal emotion that precipitates anger is often disappointment. So, instead of yelling, calmly telling an employee that you are disappointed in him may prove to be much more effective in conveying your message, and not least because anger, in whatever form it may take, is difficult for most people to listen to and embrace.

My Dad almost never yelled, but the two times in my life he told me he was disappointed in me resonated in my bones, almost literally, and here I am writing about it 30 years later. [I'm sure he was justifiably disappointed in me far more than these two times, but these were the only two times he said it out loud.] *That* is effective message delivery and, frankly, effective management. I repeat: it is okay to get angry sometimes. All I'm saying is that sometimes anger, no matter how justified, is not the best way to deliver your message or to fix the problem.

Now, let's talk about confrontation. The process itself.

There are two basic types of confrontation: impromptu confrontation and planned. Let's first discuss acts of confrontation that you plan in advance.

As discussed, one of the very most important things you can do to improve the process of confrontation is to do it long before you get angry. The second most important thing is to use a script. You owe it to yourself, the employee, and to the company not to wing it. Confrontations are unpleasant at best. Scripts make them easier, smoother, and better. Here is a generalized script I have used successfully that can make the process easier and more effective for both parties:

1) Announce the purpose of the meeting: *John, I asked you to this meeting in order to discuss your performance over the last 30 days.*

2) Then immediately state the outline for the meeting: *I will start by stating my concerns, I will tell you the basis of those concerns, I will give you my expectations, then I will give you the opportunity to ask questions or make comments.*

3) State your complaints briefly and clearly: *In the last 30 days, you have missed three deadlines, reported to work late, and had vocal confrontations with several co-workers.*

4) Ask for the employee's response (if there is no defense, proceed to #6): *Before we go any further, is there anything else you would like to say?*

5) If there is a rebuttal, ask if there are other personnel who might be able to provide information or context that would facilitate

a better understanding of the issues: *Is there information I am missing or are there people I can talk to that will help shed more light on these issues?*

6) Discuss expectations and solutions in detail
7) Discuss benefits to employee of these solutions
8) Get "buy-in" from the employee regarding solutions
9) Monitor situation
10) Reward progress or take action

The other general category of confrontation is the unplanned or impromptu confrontation. With this type, there are a few things you can try to do – before switching over to script mode – to increase the chances that a confrontation with an employee will have a more positive than negative outcome:

1) Stay calm. Even though the situation arose suddenly, you must remind yourself to stay composed. A defensive employee is not likely to listen to what you have to say

2) Put mission over emotion – stay focused on leadership and what *good* can come from the confrontation. You can't lead if you aren't in role

3) Remember to announce and label your feelings (vs. simply emoting them)

4) Don't let emotion burn the bridge – you still have a job to do. Lead, even in the midst of confrontation

5) Believe in the employee's ability to salvage things. If you enter into a confrontation expecting that it will go badly, it probably will. Allow for and *expect* success

6) Explain yourself. Even when employees are being criticized or reprimanded, articulating the logic behind your statements and assertions is more effective than emotion and any opinions not thoroughly expressed

7) Stay mindful. Watch yourself. Place your words. Be self-aware. Be a leader. *Do your job*

Confrontation is unpleasant, taxing, and is a difficult skill to master, but a leader endeavors to become proficient in this skill the same as any other.

CHAPTER 14

In Lieu of Charisma

M any people – maybe even most – believe that leaders are born. Well, sure, leaders *are* born. Some people just have what it takes to naturally lead other people. We've all seen this to be true.

Charisma is hard to come by. I can't put a percentage on it, but I would say that the percentage of people with charisma is relatively low. Do 10% of people have it? 5%? I suppose it doesn't really matter too much, as long as we agree that the number is certainly not high.

Born leaders are typically charismatic, smart, persuasive, outgoing, friendly, good communicators, confident, and a few other things here and there. And, charisma, it is not too hard to argue, seems to be one of the more compelling attributes of a leader. Charisma is just one of those things that causes people to pay attention, to be interested, to draw near. Charisma is powerful. Very. It sucks us in, and much of the time, we can't really explain why that is. Which is why it is such a significant factor in leadership – it's visceral, molecular, human. And, all it takes is a few of the more tangible leadership qualities combined with a measure of charisma in a person and suddenly you've got yourself the makings of a leader. So, yes, leaders *are* born. The question, of course, is whether leaders can be *produced* by any other traits, or combination of them, as well. My answer is yes, *absolutely*.

So, what else besides charisma causes people to follow a leader? The answer can be distilled into just three feelings or states of mind: *trust, respect,* and *admiration.* But, obviously it's what these three are built upon that is important for us to examine.

Employees and people in general have trust in and have respect and admiration for leaders who are hard workers, especially for those that work as hard as or harder than they do. Expertise is also very often a factor in whether or not people have respect and trust in their leader. Being the most learned or experienced man or woman in a given discipline is a condition that tends to cause people to listen to and follow that person. But, there is also a set of concepts that cause people to follow a leader, and for those of you truly absorbing this discussion, the answer is obvious: *ethics, reason,* and *excellence.* Because, is there really anything else worthy of following?

Sure, people want to be inspired. We all do. OK, *most* of us do, and the charismatic man or woman is often inspiring. But, what I have observed to be inspiring also are those attributes in a leader that cause employees to trust and to follow – and compelling speeches and charismatic personalities, while effective, are not the only game in town. We can't imbue or teach charisma, of course, but we can certainly teach and learn ethics, reason, and excellence. When charisma is lacking, there are many other attributes that very easily fill in gaps in charisma. Consistency, patience, respectfulness, expertise, thoroughness, loyalty, for example, while less dynamic, are ultimately just as motivating as charisma. So you weren't a born leader? No matter. Charisma without these other elements is of little value anyway, so why not focus on the more important and foundational aspects of leadership from the outset.

CHAPTER 15

People

As I said earlier, I do not find people very complicated – troublesome, quirky, inconsistent, and 43 other things, perhaps, but not terribly complicated. But, I suppose it all depends on your perspective. Mine is that employees essentially have very similar wants and needs. Sure, people are very different from each other in personality, personal preferences, idiosyncrasies, and so on, but when it comes to what people expect from a leader, the list is short and pretty easy to predict.

Most people, it's safe to say, just want to be paid a fair wage, to be provided a safe and comfortable environment in which to work, and to be shown fairness and respect by their supervisors and co-workers. In this way, people are pretty simple.

One of the clichés that tends to be repeated often where I work is that in management, 80% of the job is dealing with personnel matters, which, where I work, and I suspect in most places around the country regardless of the job, is more or less true. The corollary to this cliché is that 10% of the people are responsible for 80% of the personnel issues (although I have observed the quoted percentage to go as high as 30%, depending on the day and the level of frustration). So, the point is twofold, as you can see: one, most people are fairly simple and only want fair treatment and conditions in exchange for an honest day's work, and two, a small percentage of employees will always be difficult to please and an ever-present headache.

I come from a psychology background. Human behavior is at the forefront of most everything I think about during the day. And, while we often talk about how complicated people are and how complicated people make things at work, the truth is, if we better focused our efforts on what motivates and demotivates people, many of the seemingly complicated aspects of managing employees would be much easier. For example, an employee who is chronically late, who gives a different excuse every time is not complicated. He is very simple. Eleven different excuses doesn't make his situation or yours, as a leader, complicated at all. He is coming in late for one of just a few simple reasons, generally speaking. He doesn't want to be at work for some reason, or he has control issues and is testing you. The solution to this is simple: find out which it is and either set clear expectations and/or help him with any legitimate problem he may be having. Either way, you won't know what to do until you discuss it with him. Most of the time, the problem is what we think it is. But sometimes, the problem isn't what we thought it was at all. In both instances, though, the employee's motivation or demotivation is a common one that requires very little effort to decode.

There are very few, if any, real mysteries in human behavior, as far as I'm concerned. People are pretty darned simple when you get right down to it. All you have to do to figure them out is to talk to them – with sincerity and with the simple goal of understanding their individual perspective. Leadership, motivation, conflict resolution, and a hundred other constructs having to do with the interactions of humans all begin and end with communication.

CHAPTER 16

Communication

W hen I was in my teens, I told an adult friend of mine that being misunderstood was at the top of the list of the things I detested most – not misunderstood in the sense that I was so complicated that no one could understand me, but in the sense that being misunderstood due to poor communication and/or poor interpretation was very frustrating and unfortunate. I had this philosophy then and have it even more so now because I believe that our communications, all of them, are swatches of the original *us*. Everything we say or write represents what we think and who we are, and because this is so, accurate communications are inherently important to portraying ourselves as we truly are. It always seemed to me that there wasn't much more important in the human experience than being understood fairly and accurately by others.

Minor misunderstandings among friends, co-workers, and acquaintances happen every day. We know this from experience – the experience of finding out days, weeks, or months later after a mundane personal interaction that something you said, *or didn't say*, was misinterpreted by Person A, who told Person B, who then told you whatever that misinterpreted something was, which turned out to be something you never even *thought*, much less actually said. Typically, this occurs because of the tendency of humans to listen with a biased ear. But, it also occurs because people are not always precise in their choice of words, nor are they thorough in their explanations. Conversation, in general, is a medium of communication that is naturally prone to error, by the speaker and by the audience, due to the failings of human nature. We tend to be lazy in our listening or in our speaking, and we make faulty assumptions without taking time to get clarifications. These are common errors that are easily avoided.

Because of my dread of being misunderstood, misinterpreted, and because I think it is courteous to the listener/recipient, I have endeavored over the years to be an over-communicator, especially in my written communications. We have long since become an e-mail society, and e-mails are at the heart of our every-day communications.

I send a lot of e-mails. Every day. Some of them are personal, some of them are business in nature, some of them are informative, some of them are complimentary, funny (arguably), and social. There is a lot of power in e-mails, I have found. I have also found that one can do a lot of damage in a very short amount of space when the writer fails to take the time to communicate his intentions thoroughly. Hasty e-mails cause problems. They often lack tone. Hurried e-mails can hurt feelings, precipitate animosity, and cause unnecessary miscommunications. You may argue that you were just in a hurry, but the recipient may perceive (and often does) that your e-mail was curt, discourteous, condescending, and even disrespectful. I have made this mistake more than once due to my trying to "multi-task" or due to my decision to send a timely reply versus waiting until I had more time to send a thoughtful and thorough one. My intentions were arguably good, but the results were not.

There is almost no excuse for a rushed e-mail, especially when one is in a position of leadership. Peer to peer e-mails can get away with a little less decorum, perhaps, but when one is a leader, the effects of a poorly sent e-mail are much more damaging. Employees receiving a terse e-mail from a boss will almost always *feel* it more negatively than the same e-mail from a colleague. So, if it is worth sending, it is worth sending well. Yes, I know that people can sometimes be thin-skinned and unreasonably sensitive – that's a fact. But two wrongs don't make a right, so why not take the high road and write your e-mails thoroughly, courteously, and considerate of all possible sensitivities – because you can.

Another aspect of interactive communication that I have found to be invaluable is the practice of patient listening. I have been fortunate to have had several high-level bosses who were particularly dedicated to this principle. Their deliberate patience in listening often made the difference between a relaxed, calm, and focused presentation by a particular subordinate speaker and one that would have otherwise been rushed, nervous, and preoccupied. What a great gift it is to any employee to be heard and heard well by his boss, and the higher up a leader goes, the more important is this discipline.

Another thing I believe is very important in leadership is transparency. Transparency breeds trust and trust is at the heart of a successful leadership environment.

When leaders make decisions, I think it is important that they explain their decisions to the troops. I don't think it is necessarily an obligation of leadership, but it shows courtesy and respect, and anytime you can express such for your people, the more they will respect you. For example, you are not obligated to tell everyone why there has been a budget decrease that affects various office supplies, travel accounts, and the like, but being forthright with everyone is far more considerate of your employees than informing them by surprise. Terminations, changes in policy, and high-level discussions that will ultimately affect your employees, for example, should be communicated to the people you manage at the earliest possible time. People appreciate transparency and feel that they are just as entitled to know what may affect their work life as you are. Transparency and over-communication are nothing more than symbols of respect, and respect is always the right thing. Respect your people, let them in on your thoughts (which will remind them that they are part of the team and that their thoughts and feelings matter) and they will follow.

CHAPTER 17

Practical Doctrine

We've been dealing in a fair amount of philosophy so far. In this chapter, I want to give you something you can hold in your hand. First, is a list of traits and behaviors that make up a good employee (they share in the responsibility, too, of course) and second, is a delineation of those traits and behaviors that make up a good leader. And, at the end is a list of those things an employee has the right to expect from a leader.

<u>Traits and Behaviors of a Good Employee</u>

A good employee should –

1. Do his job
2. Cooperate with his co-workers in doing theirs
3. Cooperate with his supervisor(s)
4. Play by the rules
5. Put the mission of the company above himself
6. Strive to be the best
7. Be enthusiastic, positive, flexible, friendly, approachable, receptive
8. Follow instructions, learn the job, remain teachable, be willing to learn new things
9. Be humble, of good character, ethical, honest, direct, sincere

10. Work hard, show initiative, take pride in work, be self-motivated
11. Be respectful, courteous, kind
12. Be responsible, conscientious, reliable, trustworthy, make mature decisions, listen well
13. Be fair, logical, objective
14. Be thorough, precise, and courteous in speech, documentation, and service, be responsive, answer phones/e-mails promptly
15. Be professional, represent the company well, dress appropriate to the environment/occasion
16. Update supervisor without being prompted
17. Build relationships, be helpful to the team, volunteer for tasks
18. Be punctual, stay administratively prepared and pure
19. Ask for help when it's needed, be open to feedback and recommendations, be self-aware
20. Be a "leader in place"

Traits and Behavior of a Good Leader

A good supervisor/manager, if he is to be a good leader, should –

1. Be supportive, mentoring, inspiring; be a leader, not just a boss
2. Be honest, honorable, ethical
3. Be kind genuine, caring, compassionate, sincere
4. Be candid, straightforward, never exaggerate
5. Be approachable, available, respectful, courteous, engaged
6. Be decisive, firm, steadfast, confident
7. Be knowledgeable, experienced, or trying to learn
8. Have common sense, be discerning, logical, analytical
9. Be thorough, precise, and courteous in speech, documentation, and service
10. Be transparent in communications and decision-making

11. Be fair, objective, impartial
12. Be engaged, mission-focused, passionate, dedicated, loyal
13. Be service-oriented, selfless
14. Be trusting (non-micromanaging) of good employees, hold employees accountable to standards of good work and good conduct
15. Lead by example
16. Listen well and patiently
17. Give feedback, be appreciative of excellent performance
18. Be positive, cheerful, easy to talk to, energetic
19. Ask for feedback, be receptive to well-intended advice
20. Be timely, responsive, organized, calm
21. Never hold a meeting without a clear and meaningful goal; *not* hold a meeting when a simple e-mail or individual meeting is just as good or better

Employee Rights

An employee has the right to –

1. Fair, honest, respectful treatment by management
2. Fair, honest, respectful treatment by fellow co-workers
3. Express respectful disagreement with management without fear of retaliation
4. Be treated as a person and not just an employee
5. Be managed by a leader that will do the right thing by the employee, regardless of title, company politics, or personal politics

Rightful Employee Expectations

An employee may rightfully expect a leader to –

1. Do his job; supervise, manage, and lead his employees to meet/exceed company objectives

2. Make his expectations clear and to explain the basis/objective of those expectations
3. Provide what is needed for employees to do their jobs
4. Maintain a pleasant work environment in return for a full day's work
5. Be transparent and communicative about both successes and disappointments
6. Hold all employees accountable for their duties and responsibilities
7. Hold himself accountable for his own duties and responsibilities
8. Reward excellent performance and reprimand poor performance and conduct in all employees in a timely manner
9. Enforce company rules, policies, and regulations
10. Defend his employees when his employees are right
11. Choose what is right over self-interests

Espousing these principles openly as the new leader of a group of employees, for example, can be invaluable. It sets forth the ground rules for both parties and, most importantly, holds the manager accountable by virtue of his openly stating the rules he intends to apply to himself. If the manager succeeds in his accountability, then it will be impossible for an employee to justify any failures in his. Make yourself accountable to your employees and to yourself. State what you believe in and let everyone know it. It will cause people to trust you and it will keep you honest.

CHAPTER 18

Title Wielding and Bullying

O ne of the most common negative behaviors I have observed in those managers that lack leadership ethics is a form of bullying behavior I call "title wielding." Title wielding is the use of one's superior *title* to elicit a particular action by a subordinate employee by using it as if it were a prod or a club. It's less egregious or dramatic than bullying but falls into the same category of conduct. Typically, when a manager employs this method of "communication," the use of his title as a prod or a lever is implied by the context of the conversation. Most managers don't come straight out and say "You better do XYZ because I'm the boss." But, when they do issue an instruction or order, the tone of such, the delivery, is often more implicative of the manager's superior position than it is of the manager's superior logic, expertise, or some other factor that would naturally afford the manager a more enlightened perspective.

Title wielding often emerges in situations where there is some form of confrontation between the supervisor and the employee. However, if this is a tendency indicative of the manager's personality in general, as it often is, the behavior can show itself in any situation. For example, title wielders are often very impatient with their employees. When an employee wants to discuss something, the manager is fidgety, abrupt, or dismissive, simply because they are the boss and can get away with it. Now, I realize that many of you reading this will say this isn't a fair analysis in that sometimes employees are just wasting time, making excuses, are annoying, etc. – all valid points. Sometimes this is true. Those circumstances aside, however, there is a tendency of some managers to treat employees less patiently or respectfully than they would co-worker peers or the average acquaintance. Once the notion of title seeps into the interaction with an employee – and I do accept that it is often subconscious – leadership evaporates and the superficiality of hierarchy and the false superiority that goes with it is all that is left: *I am higher than you; therefore, my time, my thoughts, my voice are more important than yours.* Each time a manager puts his title ahead of ethics and well-applied philosophy in addressing a personnel matter with a subordinate, the employee becomes less and less trusting of the manager. This quickly leads to an ever-intensifying cycle of distrust and avoidance between the two parties, which reduces the relationship to little more than subordination. Any manager can "win" a debate with an employee by implying through word or tone that his title makes him right, but a leader persuades an employee through better analysis, better philosophy, and/or greater experience, *or* concedes to the employee on the same basis (for this, too, is leadership).

Why do some managers wield their title? Well, first, because they *can*, and often because it reduces the time required to spend with that employee (bullying, like anger, can be expeditious to the undisciplined and impatient boss), and because the manager does not respect the employee, nor does he respect the principle of fairness. *What gives a manager the right to push around an employee he does not particularly want to deal with?* His title and nothing more, because it certainly isn't ethics.

I have yet to meet a single manager that thought he or she was a bully. We've all known at least one or two over the years, but no one ever self identifies – one, because they know it is a bad thing to be, and two, because it is much more often unintentional than it is just a very bad habit. So, as you're reading this and you have any doubt about whether you are or aren't, that isn't a very good sign.

Yes, employees can be annoying, undisciplined, and difficult, but a leader has a duty to mentor, to mold, to address conflict, to remedy, to enlighten, to coach, and to motivate, even when they shouldn't have to. *Because that's the job.* Title wielding is about position and status. It presumes inequality at the outset, even though it is often subconscious. In considering this concept, ask yourself these questions:

1. Do you listen to your employees as patiently as you would to a friend over lunch?

2. When an employee disagrees, do you respond with the same respect as you would if you were talking to a peer?

3. Do you use intimidation instead of persuasion when differing with an employee?

4. Do you typically get annoyed or even angry when an employee asks "Why?"

5. Do you say "no" to new ideas more often than not, simply because it takes less effort than having a discussion?

6. Do you behave as though your title obligates you to be or *makes* you the smartest person in the room?

7. Do you treat your employees with the same sense of respect as you do your superiors?

8. Do you feel that your time is more valuable than your employees'?

9. Do you get your confidence/courage from your title or from your philosophies?

If you answered yes to any of these, then it is likely that you have, at one time or another, put your title above leadership. It's a common thing. Very. And it's very human. It just doesn't happen to be the best way of leading people.

Now let's address title wielding's bigger and uglier brother. Though the act of bullying shouldn't have much of a place in any book on leadership, I decided that I should discuss it, at least briefly, for the same reason that I believe title wielding to be worth discussing: supervisory bullying does go on, even though we all know how unfair, damaging, and wrong it is, and because it is not exactly rare.

I realize that definitions of bullying can vary from personality to personality, so I hope you will find my definitions to be reasonable and fair. I am not someone who calls being in a bad mood now and then, for example, a form of bullying. It's not. What I think of as bullying behavior by a manager is excessive and clearly oppressive. For example, excessive criticism, without a discussion of rehabilitation, is a form of bullying. Threatening, demeaning, or any other psychologically abusive behavior is bullying behavior. Sabotaging employees' work, relationships, or reputation in order to undermine them is bullying. Controlling communications by being domineering, cutting people off, and not allowing them to speak freely are all forms of bullying, especially when title makes it clear that the employee does not have a choice but to endure the interaction. Spying on employees and informing them that you are keeping watch (unrelated to ongoing punishment or rehabilitation) can be another form of bullying. Punishing an employee for something unrelated to job performance or the mission can be another form. Expecting more from an employee than is fair or reasonable, applying rules to one employee differently than they are applied to another, discounting or omitting accomplishments of an employee, and exploiting weakness and insecurities in an employee can also be forms of bullying. This is the short list, but there are many forms, and all are based on power. Bullying is in many ways the exact opposite of leadership.

Sometimes – not always – but sometimes, bullying is not about intent. Sometimes it is about the employee's perceived lack of power or options. Not everyone is equal in their ability to defend themselves, to negotiate, to explain, or defend. What one employee might perceive as a boss who is having a bad day, another employee might perceive as persecution. That's from the side of the employee. From the perspective of the manager, however, bullying can also be a form of punishment, because, sometimes, bullying *is* conscious and intentional.

Sometimes bully managers bully employees as a way of punishing them for being bad employees. Sometimes it is a passive-aggressive form, albeit an ineffective one, of trying to get an employee to behave in a better way. I'm not suggesting that all bullied employees are blameless – far from it. All I am suggesting is that bullying is bad leadership, bad management, and isn't ethical.

CHAPTER 19

Survey Results

One part of the leadership presentation I gave at work involved a brief original survey that I disseminated to more than 500 employees prior to my presentation. The first question I asked in that survey was *"What five traits/behaviors of your supervisor, or any past supervisor, do you admire the most or do you find most effective in terms of leadership?"* I also asked, *"If anything, what two things would make your supervisor a better leader?"* Though I tallied the results from these two questions separately, for purposes of the presentation, I presented the results together by rank-ordering the answers by frequency of the answers submitted.

Before I collected the results, I made predictions regarding the responses I believed I would receive, listing the first 11 traits/behaviors that I believed would result. Upon collecting the responses from over 350 responding employees, I discovered that 10 of my 11 predictions were in the top 11 responses from those employees who participated in the survey. My point in noting this is not to imply that I am smart. It is rather to affirm what I said earlier with regard to people being relatively simple (and therefore relatively easy to predict). Yes, it is possible that I was merely being intuitive about people or that I was particularly in tune with my co-workers. But I think in this instance, it is more likely that I simply channeled what it is to be an employee in general and predicted what it is that an average employee hopes to get from a decent leader. I'm not sure that takes much intuition *or* psychology. But, whatever the case, employee responses to this survey fell into 21 categories for the first question – listed below in order of the frequency in which they occurred – and in 22 categories in order of frequency in response to the second question.

Traits Admired in a Leader

1. Supportive, mentoring, inspiring
2. Honest, honorable, candid, ethical
3. Kind, genuine, caring, compassionate, sincere
4. Approachable, humble, available
5. Decisive, firm, steadfast, courageous, confident
6. Knowledgeable, experienced, has common sense, discerning, logical
7. Good communicator, transparent
8. Fair, objective, impartial
9. Engaged, employee-focused, service-oriented, selfless
10. Non-micromanaging
11. Leads by example, hard-working
12. Patient, good listener
13. Gives feedback, appreciative
14. Positive, cheerful, easy to talk to, energetic
15. Flexible
16. Passionate, dedicated to the cause
17. Calm
18. Asks for feedback/advice
19. Holds people accountable
20. Unafraid of higher-ups
21. Responsive, timely, organized

Traits Disdained in a Leader

1. Narcissistic, self-serving, takes the credit
2. Unfair, dishonest, deceitful, unethical

3. Micromanaging
4. Detached, lazy, unapproachable, negative
5. Dismissive, arrogant, condescending, disrespectful, rude
6. Biased, engages in favoritism
7. Puts business over people, stats over quality
8. Indecisive, flip-flopping, knee-jerk, fearful in decision making
9. Know-it-all, insecure, defensive, competitive with own employees
10. Holds grudges, retaliatory, vindictive, spiteful
11. Does not hold employees accountable
12. Domineering, demeaning, intimidating, bullying
13. Pleases management instead of defending own beliefs
14. Disorganized, excitable, forgetful, inept, unresponsive
15. Volatile, emotional, moody, rash, angry
16. Gossipy
17. Inflexible, does not listen to others' views, does not ask for advice or feedback
18. Unappreciative, does not offer praise or feedback, mule-driver
19. Does not mentor, is not supportive of the individual
20. Does not distribute work fairly (unfairly uses workhorses)
21. Risk-averse
22. Passive-aggressive, no conflict resolution skills

I was not surprised by anything on this list, nor were the managers to whom I gave the presentation. All of these categories seem reasonable, practical, and appropriate. Obviously, from an empirical perspective, it would be difficult to assign any significance to the responses of one small sampling of the workforce such as this one. On the other hand, after reviewing the 21 and 22 categories of responses above, I assume that the reader will find it as difficult to imagine as I that giving the same survey in any city in the U.S. would yield significantly different results. *Employees are employees are employees.*

My beliefs and convictions about leadership were formed long before I conducted the survey, so even though the results appear to align themselves well with my philosophies, to be fair, what an employee *says* he or she wants in a leader doesn't necessarily equate to what being a good leader actually is. And though in this case it does appear as though they are one and the same, I am not trying to suggest that one equals the other. I am merely presenting to you the results as they occurred.

CHAPTER 20

A Humble Heed to Executives

I n my role as a confidant and counselor to both employee, manager, and executive over many years, I have observed a condition that has been quite consistent regarding upper managers' perceptions of their lower managers. This phenomenon is something I call the "fence post phenomenon," a phenomenon by which upper managers tend to perceive and judge their mid-level and lower-level managers based solely on the interactions they have with them. That is, their view of these managers is limited to what rises *up*. What they *don't* see is what goes on from the mid-level position down below to those employees the managers supervise. The majority of what upper managers see is the fence post above the ground. What they don't see is the condition of the post down below.

A wooden fence post can stand for many years through all kinds of weather and still look pretty good above ground. But, 10-20 years on, the post beneath the ground is a much different view. I won't belabor the fence post analogy with unnecessary descriptions of decay, bugs, and other unpleasantness, but suffice it to say that the part of the post that rises above the ground is far prettier than the post that exists below it. I have observed the same to be true within the hierarchy of management.

Upper-level managers are typically (and innocently) insulated and every upper manager I have discussed this with admits it, as is the nature of things where most of us work. Upper-level managers have high-level functions to perform, and, by design, they have lower-level managers to perform the functions they do not have time to. Lower-level managers, are, therefore, assessed primarily on what they present to upper-level managers in both work product and in social-business interactions, but what upper managers rarely see is how their managers actually "lead" their employees. Sure, they may see the "numbers" and a given demeanor, but the numbers and the demeanor they see often tell only part of the story.

I work at a place that has a lot of self-motivated people. Where I work, the numbers are often at least as reflective of the employees' performance as they are of the supervisors' leadership. Put another way, a less-than-competent supervisor can easily present good numbers to his superiors because the employees on his team are doing good work *independent* of their supervision.

What upper managers rarely get to see is the day-to-day interactions their managers have with their employees, and almost never anonymously. When upper managers do check in on their subordinate managers and those they supervise, *the observer effect* naturally kicks in and the managers obviously put their best foot forward, such that whatever their superiors observe is undoubtedly intended to make themselves look as good as they can possibly look. I'm not suggesting that supervisors are necessarily being deceitful. All I am saying is that it is human nature to be on our best behavior when the boss is around.

So, between office walk-arounds by the big bosses that yield understandably artificial observations and the meetings and conferences that these bosses have with these same managers, upper-level bosses are very often left with impressions of their managers that are considerably better than these impressions might be with the staff of those managers.

Upper managers owe it to the people they lead to be thoroughly informed of the well-being of *all* their employees. Yes, employee welfare is the responsibility of everyone in the chain; however, I believe that – and, again, every manager I have talked to about this agrees – the man or woman in charge is the ultimate caretaker of employee morale. And although it takes some extra effort, I have found that there is no better way of learning of the comfort, happiness, and mental health of employees than by asking them directly. When upper managers fail to truly know the treatment of employees by their managers, the people often go unheard and unprotected.

Many managers I have broached this topic with have asked why employees didn't just come to them directly when there were supervisory problems, somewhat naively believing that complaining to an upper-level boss should be relatively easy to do, was welcomed, and was in some ways their (the employees') obligation.

The truth is, the average employee is not comfortable talking to an upper manager about their boss at all. "Jumping the chain," making an appointment with a boss several levels above them, and not knowing how the meeting might turn out are all intimidating conditions to the average worker, even if they believe the boss would be sincere in hearing them out. I have seen this to be true many times, even with the best of bosses. Secondly, most employees fear that even if their complaints are heard and addressed, the possibility of retaliation by their first-line supervisor makes the thought of complaining seem like a very misguided proposition.

Leadership is about solving problems. The day soldiers stop bringing you their problems is the day you have stopped leading them. They have either lost confidence in that you can help or concluded that you do not care. Either case is a failure of leadership.

– General Colin Powell

Upper managers are right when they say that they can't fix a problem if they don't know what the problem is. But I do not believe that it is incumbent on those with the least power to raise the alarm. I believe instead that it is incumbent on those with the most power and the most responsibility, the top leaders, to proactively ask if all is well.

Good leaders do not wait for the fence post to break before they start asking about rot beneath the surface. Good leaders know that there is sometimes more to the story than that which rises up from the ground, realizing well that there is sometimes a different personality, a different presentation that exists between a mid-level manager and his people, a presentation that cannot effectively be observed from the position of upper management without going the extra mile.

Good leaders ask questions. They don't assume the numbers tell the whole story, and they don't assume all their managers treat their employees as well as they treat them. Leaders, if you want to know how your managers are doing, all you have to do is ask your employees. Give them a safe and confidential environment in which to speak – whether in the form of a confidential survey, a private conference, an e-mail, or in a simple conversation in the hallway – and they will tell you what you need to know for the good of the company, themselves, and you. Much of the time, things will run smoothly, but sometimes, when there are a few managers lacking leadership skills and leadership ethics, top cover from upper manager and executives can mean the difference between happy employees and miserable ones. I have seen it many times.

One last thing on the subject of "top cover." Leaders, please remember that if you work at a place that has routine turn-over in the management ranks, including at your own level, employees are going to be reluctant to be very disclosive with complaints about their supervisors because their top cover, namely you, might not be there forever, while the supervisor who is the subject of their complaint just might be. You might very well be willing, capable, and eager to make management corrections in favor of employees, and the employees might sincerely believe this. But, if they know that you, their managerial guardian, will be leaving in two years and their boss is a "lifer," you should not be surprised to find employee eagerness to report complaints anemic, at best. Employees have to survive, and it is not easy to survive at work if the person you have complained about – no matter how righteously – is your boss and there is no one above him that is left to hold him accountable. In such a circumstance, employees have a very angst-ridden dilemma: tell the big boss, hope it sticks for a few years until it can be successfully revisited with the next big boss (if they are so lucky); or, say nothing and do their best to ride it out in pained silence.

I have had this very conversation with numerous leaders over the last many years. All of them appeared to hear me and seemed to understand and acknowledge the genuineness of the problem. Some of those executives took action and fixed the problem permanently, others addressed the problem, only to learn that the problem reared its head again after they had gone, and others attempted to address the problem but never really found or were able to actuate a sustainable solution.

It is obviously impossible for leaders to fight these battles once they have moved on, so there are really only two things that can be done before a leader decides to depart: he can remedy the problem before he goes, or, barring an immediate solution, he can ensure that before he departs, he has instilled in those around him – all those that are responsible for the company and its employees – a culture that reflects his own leadership belief system. If the belief system he has established has been, in fact, *established*, then the need for a single executive to fix managerial problems will be obviated, as leadership ethics will be pervasive enough there for the next man or woman in line to provide a solution.

So there is my charge to executives: solve problems before you leave, but in case you can't, be sure to provide the proper training and instill the proper principles in your people, so that you aren't the sole linchpin holding the entire operation together.

CHAPTER 21

Management Styles

I do not believe in the concept of management *styles*. It's a concept that just never rang true for me. I have never accepted that there are actual and distinct "styles" of management. There are, of course, an almost infinite number of personalities within the population of managers, some of which could be generalized to between five and 10 general mannerisms, perhaps, but I do not believe that there are any real management approaches that are systematic and disciplined enough to be called "styles." I freely admit that I know very little about the topic in the academic sense, but I am aware that it is a relatively common topic in business-themed management books. I just happen to perceive these to be more focused on method than on principle, and I'm not convinced that the *methods* offer any genuine distinctions.

I realize, of course, that these statements will undoubtedly annoy all the learned and capable men and women who have written books on the topic and perhaps even some of you who have spent time reading them. I am not trying to be original, rebellious, or disrespectful. I simply felt that I should address a topic that many people reading about leadership may want to discuss, as both terms, *leadership* and *management*, are often mentioned in the same breath.

When asked recently (and I really was) what I considered my management style to be, I said, "doing the right thing." I assure you, I was not trying to sound virtuous. I was merely professing the belief that for me, there is no management "style" outside a focus on *ethics, reason*, and *excellence*. Trying to do things *rightly, wisely*, and *well*, therefore, is my style of leadership/management.

When I hear people say in a particular circumstance, "Yeah, y'know, that's just not my management style," I shake my head quietly because what people really seem to mean when they say this is that they don't have the energy, the courage, or the humility to do it the right way. My internal response to this all-too-common reply, while admittedly sarcastic, is "so hard work, decency, and guts just isn't your *management style*, huh?" How unfortunate.

A few years ago, I was talking to a manager about "management styles." He told me he was about to scold a lower-level manager that worked for him, a guy who had made a decision regarding an employee that the manager didn't agree with, telling me that the manager he supervised "doesn't have a very good management style." I asked him why he was going to criticize this supervisor, and he told me he thought the supervisor would be viewed by his employees as "weak" once they learned that he had allowed an employee to "win" a debate with him, resulting in a change in business process agreed to by the supervisor. When I asked my friend if past reviews of this supervisor by his employees had reflected that the supervisor was perceived as weak, the manager smiled uncomfortably, as if caught, and admitted they had not. I added that I also did not perceive this supervisor to be weak, and that even if he were, the decision that he made appeared to be quite logical, and because it seemed so, I politely appealed to the manager to go easy on him. Somewhat hesitantly, the manager asked me if I agreed with the supervisor's decision, and I told him that I did. When I asked the manager why *he* did not agree with the decision, he said, "I don't necessarily disagree with his decision, but I don't think it is a good idea to let employees [subordinates] win debates. "That's just not my style. It looks bad," he said. I suggested to the manager that, indeed, weakness itself in a supervisor does, of course, look bad, but that the very act of agreement with an employee, or even concession, is not the equivalent of submission due to a lack of competence, courage, or wisdom. Naturally, I argued the reverse in that by listening to his subordinate's ideas and agreeing with them, the supervisor showed true leadership by being secure, mature, smart, and responsible enough to do the right, wise, and most productive thing he could do for the company, *and* looked all the more *strong* to his employees for doing so. Whether the manager took my recommendation to heart or not, I do not know. What I do know is that making decisions against your own better judgment for the sake of appearing in control is not a legitimate *style* of management.

I freely accept that every manager will naturally have his or her own personality and manner of communication – hopefully, it is obvious that it is not my intent to try to prescribe style. To be very frank, as someone philosophizing on leadership, all I am concerned with is a focus on leadership *principles*. How each leader comes to apply these principles, by what actions, behaviors, and modes of expression are up to him or her. In the end, as long as the boxes for *ethics*, *reason*, and *excellence* are checked, *how* one checks them is not particularly important.

One final comment about management styles. While I do not like the concept of a static style of management, per se, I do think there are times when style *is* important in relation to one particular aspect of management as it applies to the management of the individual nature of each employee.

While people may be simple (not complex), they are all unique. Every employee has his own features and peculiarities, preferences and foibles. Therefore, the best management style is the one that motivates *that* individual. So, having a management style, you see, actually works against you. If *your* management style is the focus, then the individual employee's psyche isn't. People are different and should be managed and led accordingly.

Some employees are motivated by simple trust, some by awards, some by private recognition and a quiet pat on the back, some must be motivated by expressed disappointment, others by scolding and punishment. Everyone is different, so adopting a single *style* of management doesn't make much sense to me. Not all ailments respond to a single kind of medicine, nor do all employees respond to a single kind of management. Tailoring your leadership, your words, your delivery, your considerations to the *individual* are the best ways to motivate a particular employee. In the realm of leadership, the employees' needs are far more important than any preset style of a given manager. Adaptation and flexibility with employee personalities are imperative to successful leadership.

CHAPTER 22

Correcting Leadership Errors

E ven the very best leaders make mistakes. Luckily, the formula for correcting leadership errors is just as simple and effective as is the formula for being a leader: 1) A leader should acknowledge that a mistake has been made, admit where the fault lies, and apologize to those affected – because nothing is more endearing than humility; 2) He should make every effort to correct the error (retract, rescind, rework, etc.) as soon as is feasible – because nothing engenders admiration more than a person who rushes to correct his mistakes; 3) He should make himself accountable to his employees – in the spirit of transparency – by publically endeavoring not to repeat the error – because nothing is more facilitating of trust than shining the light on one's own fallibility and vowing not to make the same mistake again.

Just because "it seems to be working" doesn't mean it is. First, you are most likely biased about your own leadership "style." Second, who is going to tell you if it isn't working? Third, production in and of itself is not proof of leadership effectiveness, nor is the fact that "the bosses are happy" with you.

Unless you are getting leadership assessments or performance appraisals from the employees themselves, it would be very difficult to know whether your leadership methods are successful or not. Just because your superiors think you are doing a good job doesn't mean that your subordinates do. Good leaders, though, are able to satisfy both sides of the house and actually care about the employee side as much as the executive side. True leaders want to do right by both contingents and true leaders can. Do both management and staff like and respect you? Are your "popularity" numbers as high as your production numbers? No, of course, leadership should not be focused on popularity; on the other hand, popularity is not such a bad construct to be mindful of either. Being likable is always a good thing.

Just the other day someone came to me and in explaining how they came to talk to me for advice, they said that before seeking me out they asked someone they knew their opinion of me. That person told my visitor that they did not particularly like me but they did respect me. Although for several different reasons (none of which are important to the context of this discussion) this did not hurt my feelings, I did make note of it, thinking to myself that, barring any personal issues that may have been involved, it should almost always be possible to be both liked and respected by most people. The person who had come to talk to me did not say who his friend was and I did not ask. There could have been ten reasons why the person didn't like me. Some may have been legitimate; some may not have been – it is not for me to judge. We simply can't know, nor is it relevant to the present point. What is relevant, I think, is that being liked, rather having *likability*, is just as important as respectability and productivity. I'm not suggesting it should be the primary emphasis of a leader, but it *is* important. Can a leader be effective, if he is not likable? I do not think so. And, even if you think this isn't true, I think it is easy to argue that a leader can be far more effective if he is liked.

Leadership means making people feel good.

– Jean Chrétien

CHAPTER 23

Self-Evaluation

A s you go to work each day, it is good to remind yourself of your duty as a leader. From time to time, asking yourself these questions about the quality of your leadership may help you stay on track:

- Are you a leader or just a supervisor/manager?
- Do you use your title to serve or just to administer and control?
- Is leadership your daily focus?
- Are you supportive, mentoring, inspiring of your employees?
- Do you have integrity? Are you ethical, honest, candid?
- Are you genuine, caring, compassionate, kind, sincere?
- Are you approachable, humble, available, welcoming?
- Are you discreet in your dealings with employees?
- Are you decisive, steadfast, firm, courageous, confident in your decision-making?
- Are you knowledgeable, do you use common sense, logic, and judgment?
- Are you a good communicator? Are you transparent in your interactions with employer and employees?
- Are you fair, objective, and impartial?
- Are you fully engaged, mission-focused, service-oriented, selfless?
- Are you trusting of good employees, non-controlling?
- Do you lead by example? Are you consistently hard-working?
- Are you a patient, sincere listener?

- Do you give constructive feedback and recognition?
- Are you positive, cheerful, easy to talk to, energetic?
- Are you flexible, willing to listen to others' views?
- Do you deal with things calmly?
- Do you seek feedback and recommendations?
- Are you respectful, courteous, and professional?
- Do you hold employees accountable who are not doing their jobs, or are disruptive or problematic?
- Are you confident in your dealings with managers above you? Do you put principle over politics? Do you say what needs to be said?
- Are you timely and responsive, organized, efficient?

Or, could you change a few things?

- Are you just looking for the next job? Have you lost interest in the company and the mission?
- Are you always fair and ethical?
- Do you micromanage?
- Are you detached, unengaged, unapproachable?
- Are you dismissive, angry, disrespectful?
- Do you show favoritism, bias?
- Do you make decisions based on knee-jerk reactions or fear?
- Are you indecisive? Do you flip-flop or have difficulty making decisions in general?
- Do you put business over people? Are you more statistic-focused than leadership-focused?
- Are you a know-it-all? Are you defensive, critical, resentful of talented, experienced employees?
- Do you hold grudges? Are you retaliatory, vindictive, spiteful?
- Do you use your title to be domineering, demeaning, intimidating?
- Do you defer to management even when you are right?
- Are you disorganized, excitable, forgetful?

- Are you sometimes volatile, rude, emotional, moody?
- Do you gossip, "talk out of school"?
- Do you discount employees' ideas in favor of your own simply because you're the boss?
- Do you ever ask for feedback or advice?
- Do you recognize employee accomplishments?
- Do you encourage employees, mentor, and show them the way?
- Do you assign most of the work to a few and avoid dealing with poor performers?
- Are you afraid of risk because you lack confidence in yourself?
- Are you passive-aggressive because you do not know how to deal with conflict?

Are you truly dedicated to self-evaluation, to honing your leadership skills, to maintaining self-awareness even in the face of tedium, discomfort, and frustration? Do you really want to know if you are doing a good job? Do you really want to be honest with yourself? If so, print these questions and check the list every six months. Great leaders check themselves in order to stay true and on course. A leader is not what he believes in; he is what he does. Most all of us *believe* in doing the right thing, but the only thing that really counts is actually doing it.

CHAPTER 24

Growth and Evolution

W here I work, surveys are conducted annually by our main office to assess the effectiveness of all levels of management. These surveys, as you can imagine, are both eagerly anticipated and dreaded, depending on who you are, and are the talk of the office for a few weeks every year once the results are announced. The surveys are completed by the majority of employees and include ratings and assessments of those managers in each employee's chain of command.

Most managers do well, a portion are middling, and some aren't very good at all. A few years ago, two middle-level managers came to me independent of each other and asked me to review the results of their assessments by those they supervised and to provide them with an analysis.

The decision to open the books and to let me see inside took guts. Allowing me to see their ratings and the section with personal comments made by numerous employees was not something that was easy for either of these managers, but they did it, and I'm sure it was not very comfortable. However, they were interested enough in their role as leaders to ask for an objective, third-party opinion for the sake of trying to improve themselves. Providing analysis of these annual surveys was not a function that I had performed in the past and was not necessarily in my job description, so when these two approached me with their request, I was surprised and impressed.

You want to be a leader? Seek feedback from your employees. If you don't have a program in place for performance appraisals, get one. It is an invaluable tool, if the notion of improving the leadership skills in your organization is something to which you are truly dedicated. Assessment of leaders should be conducted by those above *and* below, but especially by those below. As mentioned earlier, the fence post phenomenon will likely produce higher ratings from superiors than will evaluations from subordinates, so if you really want to know how you are doing, ask those you lead. Then, ask a third-party, an advisor, someone who is not in your chain. Outside observers often afford a more accurate view of your performance than either your superiors or your subordinates can or will. People who truly want to grow and evolve as leaders ask for criticism. Yes, it can be unpleasant, but true leaders are more eager to improve than they are averse to the emotional cost of improvement.

Continue to work on your game. If you are good in a particular area of leadership, make sure you don't allow that area to slip. If you are weak in a few other areas, focus on those and bring them up to the level of your more natural aptitudes. I'm loath to use a golf analogy, but I must admit that one is apropos here. If you are really good at driving off the tee, spend just enough time on driving to maintain your level of skill. But, if your short game is a problem, spend most of your time on that, seeking out people who can help you improve. The essence of growth and evolution in leadership is two things: humility and a dissatisfaction with being good enough. True leaders continue to improve, which is the epitome of *excellence.*

CHAPTER 25

Unasked is Uninformed

Another common tendency I have observed in management and one that has been echoed by many others I have talked to over the last 20-plus years is one that is as detrimental to managers as it is to their employees. And that is the failure to ask questions.

Some time back, a friend of mine in another office was expressing frustration about a manager who was in a discussion with several other managers regarding proposed policy changes. The manager in question was advocating for a major change in policy, advancing several reasons why he thought the changes would be helpful only to be rebutted by the other managers with reasons that were more informed, and, therefore, more logical than his own. Each time he presented his perspective, he was met with greater elucidation. "I don't think you have an understanding of the policy and its intent. There is a reason this policy is in place. Do you not know the history here?" And, of course, he did not know because he did not first ask. In the end, after being informed of the value of the policy, the manager humbly conceded, but not before there was unnecessary debate borne of his impulse to move things along with the weight of his title instead of the natural propulsion that is lent by knowledge. I have observed this many, many times: with title often comes an increased urge to use that title to bypass discussion. Because title *can*, in fact, be used to expedite business processes and avoid more in-depth examination, it often is so used. And while there is a time and a place for quick decisions, I believe that using title for this purpose too liberally is a disservice to the company and employees alike.

Title is often earned and well-deserved, but it is also a privilege and a responsibility, and more than anything else, I believe that it represents an increased opportunity to serve. Indeed, title has the *license* to dispense with inquiry and examination in favor of a quicker resolution, but I do not believe it has the inherent *justification* to do so.

It is only human, as title increases, to feel less obligated to engage in the act of consideration. The higher you go, the fewer people you have to answer to and the fewer opinions you are beholden to consider. But, I submit that obligation and responsibility, in this context, are at opposite ends of the spectrum of consideration. True, as one climbs the ranks, there is less obligation to hear others' opinions, but I believe that as *obligation*, per se, may go down, *responsibility* to do so should go up. Why? Because the more you know, the better leader you can be.

Relatedly, I have also found it very uncommon, inexplicably so, for those with title to ask for insights and recommendations from those without title. There is often a great depth of institutional knowledge (and often wisdom) in those who have been around for a long time. Yet, it is common for those in management to consult primarily with other managers in seeking guidance or conferring on matters of office operations. True, it is only natural for employees at all levels to mix with their peer group, as opposed to going outside their hierarchical stratum for consultation, but failing to do so is often responsible for decisions that are made without important facts.

I have known more than a few long-time employees who had far more institutional knowledge than their supervisors. Sometimes experience is more important than IQ, degrees, or rank. Sometimes the 25-year employee with no title knows more than the five-year supervisor, simply because he or she has seen a particular predicament and consequence before. Rank does not automatically imbue one with wisdom, obviously. If title were granted only to those who had first increased their IQ and wisdom, there would be scant few poor leaders, but we all know this is not the case. Many a manager has had the resource of a knowledgeable and experienced employee available to him but failed to avail himself of the employee merely because he was not part of the management structure. On the other hand, I have observed a few excellent leaders who *have* ventured outside their ranks and asked for the opinions of those who have had more exposure to a given set of circumstances, and in witnessing these occasions, I have seen a number of poor decisions prevented – and all it took was a step across the invisible line. Senior employees, the secretary, the guy down the hall, the maintenance man – often these non-managers know things that are of real value. Most of the time all it takes to mine their knowledge is to devote an extra few minutes to solicit their opinion. It is often a shame and a loss when leaders fail to solicit ideas outside their ranks.

CHAPTER 26

Mistakes

I have made many mistakes as a leader. I have sometimes failed to be aware of my persona such that I was less approachable than I wanted to be and should have been. I have sometimes been too harsh in my delivery when confrontations, criticism, or reprimands were conducted, failing to remember at that moment that correction and problem-solving are more important than criticism or being right. I have sometimes been too sure of myself, wrongly assuming subconsciously that past performance (mine) was a guarantee of future results (perfect decisions). I have sometimes chosen, in the heat of the moment, to win, as it were, rather than to persuade and bring along. I have sometimes allowed pride to get in the way of good philosophy (ironically, my own). I have sometimes hurt feelings needlessly, though unintentionally, in the name of good philosophy, because I failed to stay mindful of the fact that gentleness is very often a higher ethic than logic. I have many times been less patient than I knew to be and easily could have been. I have sent e-mails and had phone conversations too hastily, without being sufficiently sensitive to the needs and feelings of the other party. I have sometimes failed to be kind, allowing frustration or anger to betray my principles. I have made many other mistakes, too, of course, but I promised to make this book short...

Leaders make mistakes. They are human, and there is nothing more fallible than a human, so being a perfect leader, while the right and proper goal, just isn't attainable. The important thing, the thing that affords all of us the ability to improve as leaders, is the self-awareness that allows us to admit to our mistakes and to try to prevent them. It is okay to make mistakes in leadership as long as you understand when and why you make them and endeavor both to correct them and not to repeat them.

A man should never be ashamed to own he has been in the wrong, which is but saying, in other words, that he is wiser today than he was yesterday.

– Alexander Pope

CHAPTER 27

Kindness

True kindness, like leadership, is a mindset, a way of life, and a daily commitment. Yes, it is an *ethic*, but it is far more than that. Kindness in the heart of a leader can cause one who may lack other attributes to be a leader who is trusted, admired, and respected, and a person people will follow. And *that* is the name of the game.

Several years ago, I was talking to a manager about another manager I had met in another office. In the telling of my story, I had apparently used the word "nice" several times to describe him, and at one point the manager I was speaking to interrupted and said in a slightly annoyed way, "Why is everything always about 'nice' with you?" My answer was immediate and a bit on the scolding side. "Because it's important," I said. The manager waved his hand in mild exasperation and changed the subject. As you might've guessed, this manager was not particularly concerned with being nice himself, and people often commented on the fact.

No, being nice may not be *the* main thing, but it is *one* of the main things. Indeed, it is one of the greatest things a leader can be. People love *nice*. We talk about people that are nice all the time. In fact, if you think about it for a moment, I'm sure you will acknowledge that it is one of the first things a person says when describing someone to another (whether or not that particular person is nice).

People are naturally drawn to beauty, intelligence, honesty, charm, wit, pleasantness, and other inherently appealing human characteristics, but kindness, *niceness* may be the most powerful of them all.

If you want to lead people, truly lead them, do your best to be kind as often as you can. It is persuasive and compelling, good and right, and your employees will respond positively to it. Guaranteed.

I've always felt it very important to give compliments to employees. In fact, I've made it a habit for many years now because I think it is both kind *and* fruitful. Compliments make people feel good. They make people feel noticed. They make people happy. Compliments are also bonding. Very few things that cost so little bring two people to an increased sense of connection and consideration quicker than a sincere compliment, especially when they are written down (the permanence of a written compliment has ten times the impact of a spoken one). There's not a much better feeling as an employee than getting an e-mail or a letter from your boss commending and appreciating you on a job well done. You want your people to do a good job? Let them know that you noticed the good job they are doing and they will continue to serve you well.

I used to have a boss that went to every retirement in the office, no matter where it was held, whether he knew that person well or not. I always admired him for that because it often took up many hours of his day or night, because he often did *not* know the person very well (and, thus, could not possibly have gotten anything from it in return), and because it made the person retiring feel special because the big boss remembered him or her and cared enough to say a final thank you. It was a salute, a gesture of respect, and a selfless act of kindness. By showing respect for one employee, he also showed respect for all employees, and that kind of message pays real dividends when one is trying to be a good leader.

Of course, none of this is to say that a leader can't also be firm, demanding, or even stern. There are many times and places for taking people to task, enforcing the rules, holding people accountable, making reprimands, expressing disappointment, and so on. I'm not suggesting that leaders are obligated to be carefree and mirthful. What I am saying is that a thread of kindness woven through the fabric of your daily leadership is both a good thing and a productive one. Be kind. It costs very little and is good for morale *and* business.

Wherever there is a human being, there is an opportunity for a kindness.

– Lucius Annaeus Seneca

Conclusion

Whether this book makes any difference at all in your application of leadership will come down to pride. The good kind *and* the bad kind.

Yes, *pride*. If you truly care about becoming a true leader or improving the leadership skills you already have, the only thing that will allow you to use this book as a vehicle for that purpose is humility. If you are humble, you will be open-minded enough to see that the principles discussed here are intuitive and natural, if not self-evident. Leadership based on ethics, reason, and excellence is a formula that works and works every time. I didn't invent the "science" or the components. I just put the elements of the formula together based on what I have observed is successful when there is consistent application of all three of these parts.

Here's the thing about *negative* pride: It tends to cloud people's vision, self-awareness, and honesty. For instance, many well-intended leaders will defend their failures by saying they "have a good heart." Being good-hearted is obviously a good thing, but being a leader is about much more than that. The truth is, being "good-hearted" is what allows the majority of us to forgive ourselves for our failures. No, having good intentions is *not* enough. Not nearly.

The boot maker who says, "Yes, but I *intended* to make the stitch straighter and the leather more supple," is just as much to blame for faulty boots as the slip-shod boot maker who has always been content with mediocre workmanship. Leadership, *real* leadership, is a craft, and the best leaders commit themselves daily to expert craftsmanship. Good intentions do not make the perfect boot. Devotion, integrity, and a spirit of excellence do. The *bad* form of pride makes excuses for an imperfect boot: *"I didn't have enough time." "Most boots aren't as good as these even with the flaw." "I've had other things on my mind." "People were breaking my concentration."*

Being good-hearted and well-intended are not excuses for lack of focus, dedication, and commitment to excellence, yet most of the less-than-effective managers I have known give themselves a pass because they *meant well*. To these, I must ask, "Who *doesn't* mean well?" Leadership is duty and duty is action, but good intentions are nothing more than lip service paid to that in which you profess to believe. Leadership ethics are *daily decisions*, commitments to a belief system. Title does not define your status as a leader; your actions do.

If you're not a certified, professional mechanic, you're just a guy who works on cars. And, if you aren't a leader, a man or woman dedicated daily to the *craft* of leadership, you're just a supervisor. Almost anyone can supervise; only leaders make a real difference. Be worthy of the men and women following you. Make a difference. The formula is simple. All you have to do is the right thing: ethics, reason, and excellence will show you the way every time.

Acknowledgements

I would like to say thank you to three groups of people. First, to the many close friends, teachers, mentors, and family members I have had the true pleasure of living life with through the years. You have served as role models for me from my youth to the present day and cared about me. I have been very fortunate to have had so many people around me who have been good and kind and who have not only tolerated my intensely (exasperatingly) philosophical and analytical ways, but who have encouraged them, giving me the confidence to know that the things I believed in were, in fact, the right things all along.

The second group are the many fine leaders for whom I have worked or have had the privilege of observing. You have helped me to construct a composite of what it is to be a true leader, a composite I hope I have been able to translate to the page. I have been blessed with your generous association and tutelage and inspired by your commitment to leadership.

Lastly, thank you to the friends and family who helped me with the writing of this book: Cheryl, Dave, Janice, JDB, Jones, Todd, Karen. Your thoughtful and honest critique, reinforcement, and kindness toward me in a very personal and devoted way helped to make this book far better than it would have been (had I not forced you to get involved).

Thank you, all.

References

Angelou, Maya. Goodreads.com

Aristole. BrainyQuote.com

Bresch, Heather. December 7, 2014. 95quotes.com

Chrétien, John Jacques Jean. *Oxford Dictionary of Quotations by Subject, Second Edition, 2010.* First quoted in the Toronto Star, June 7, 1984

Da Vinci, Leonardo. BrainyQuote.com

Hopper, Grace. AZ Quotes.com

Kroc, Ray. BrainyQuote.com

Lamb, Charles. *Oxford Dictionary of Quotations by Subject, Second Edition, 2010*

Pope, Alexander. *Oxford Dictionary of Quotations by Subject, Second Edition, 2010.* First quoted in *Miscellanies Volume II, 1727, Thoughts on Various Subjects*

Powell, Colin A. Brainy Quote.com. Originally quoted in *My American Journey, 1995,* Powell, Colin A. and Persico, Joseph, Ballantine Books

Seneca, Lucius Anneaus. Inc.com

Updike, John. izQuotes.com. Originally quoted in *They Thought They Were Better*, Stacks, John F., July 21, 1980, TIME Magazine

CPSIA information can be obtained
at www.ICGtesting.com
Printed in the USA
LVHW01s2349060618
579904LV00035B/626/P

9 781457 560927